$\sim 30)$

IMAGINOLOGY

Leland Frederick Cooley

Prentice-Hall, Inc., Englewood Cliffs, New Jersey 07632

Library of Congress Cataloging in Publication Data

Cooley, Leland Frederick.
   Imaginology.

   Includes index.
   1. Success.   2. Imagery (Psychology)   3. Subconscious-
ness.   4. Prayer.   5. Belief and doubt.   6. Faith.
I. Title.
BF637.S8C655   1984   158'.1   84-9957
ISBN 0-13-451386-X
ISBN 0-13-451378-9 (A Reward book : pbk.)

10   9   8   7   6   5   4   3   2   1

Editorial/production supervision: Marlys Lehmann
Cover design: Hal Siegel
Manufacturing buyer: Pat Mahoney

ISBN 0-13-451386-X

ISBN 0-13-451378-9 {A REWARD BOOK : PBK.}

This book is available at a special discount when ordered in
bulk quantities. Contact Prentice-Hall, Inc., General
Publishing Division, Special Sales, Englewood Cliffs, N.J. 07632.

Prentice-Hall International, Inc., *London*
Prentice-Hall of Australia Pty. Limited, *Sydney*
Prentice-Hall Canada Inc., *Toronto*
Prentice-Hall of India Private Limited, *New Delhi*
Prentice-Hall of Japan, Inc., *Tokyo*
Prentice-Hall of Southeast Asia Pte. Ltd., *Singapore*
Whitehall Books Limited, *Wellington, New Zealand*
Editora Prentice-Hall do Brasil Ltda., *Rio de Janeiro*

*With love for Regina
and Elizabeth and Mike—
and in loving friendship
for David and Betsy and Scott
and Brad*

OTHER BOOKS BY THE AUTHOR:

The Run for Home
God's High Table
The Richest Poor Folks
The Trouble with Heaven
Condition Pink
California
The Art Colony
The Dancer

Contents

Preface

To begin with . . .

Have you ever wondered why some people always seem to attract *good luck*, while others seem to be born to experience bad luck?

Have you ever wondered why some people always seem to breeze through life, while others plod along on a treadmill, getting nowhere?

Have you ever wondered why some people seem to attract money, while others seem never to have enough for even the simplest pleasures?

Have you ever wondered why some people seem to enjoy radiant good health, while others seem to suffer from ailments or misfortunes, one right after another?

Have you ever wondered why some people attract wonderful, "upbeat" friends, while others go through life as "downbeat" loners?

If you have, think about this:

Every single human being, regardless of race, color, religion, or economic status, possesses a God-given power.

If you have used that power positively you are happy, healthy, and successful.

If you experience lack in your life you have not yet learned to accept that power and use it properly.

What a pity! Truly a pity, for it's so easy to turn that magic switch in your brain from *Off* to *On*.

The power, so easy to switch to *On*, lies in your "middle mind," your subconscious mind, the miracle machine that automatically keeps your physical self functioning (even when you are unconscious) and, according to the way you program it, makes you the person you are.

Let me take a moment here to say this: This book, *Imaginology*, is not intended as a substitute for the skilled professional therapy that many people need when, for one reason or another, their thought patterns and the emotions they generate have been so distorted that severe psychological damage has been done that can be repaired only by highly trained practitioners who understand the subtle and labyrinthine nature of the subconscious mind.

On the contrary, *Imaginology* shows you how to avoid being in the limbo of prolonged negative thinking that can lead to distorted lives.

Imaginology is the simple science of managing your middle mind so that it will manifest in your life those good things you dream of having.

There is no mystery about it. Without exception, everybody uses imaginology in one form or another every hour of every day.

On the following pages you will learn to use this power consciously, positively, to avoid the pitfall of negative thinking, to change yours into the most exciting and rewarding life you can imagine.

It is not a simplistic principle. It is a *profound but simple* principle—and it always works!

ACKNOWLEDGMENTS

There are so many to whom I owe a debt for the understanding they have given me. To acknowledge them all would require a book in itself.

When I was a very young newsman on Radio Station KNX in Hollywood, the door was first opened to me by Dr. Ernest Holmes, founder of The Institute of Religious Science and School of Philosophy.* He became my mentor and friend. It was he who

*Now *The Church of Religious Science.*

started me on my way by publishing my first writing attempt in *Science of Mind* magazine.

No less do I owe a special debt of gratitude to Seth and to Jane Roberts, through whom he speaks—and to Robert Butts, who so meticulously records all that is said so that the door to understanding may be opened wider still. Herewith, those debts of gratitude, and all of the others, are lovingly acknowledged.

*"You are as young as your faith,
as old as your doubt;
as young as your self-confidence,
as old as your fear;
as young as your hope,
as old as your despair . . ."*

General Douglas MacArthur
on his 75th birthday.

1

The Miracle
of Imaginology

*Imagination, among all of God's gifts
to mankind, is the richest
and most unique . . . and it was given
to man alone.*

*W*e are all born to be winners! There's no such thing as a "born loser."

In your imagination you possess one of the greatest powers on earth. It is a power that can bring into your life all the good things you need and have always wished for.

All this can happen the minute you discover the simple secret of using the God-given gifts that lie in your conscious mind and in your miraculous mental servant, your subconscious mind.

Actually, we use these powers constantly. Every thought, every wish, every hope, every desire, makes use of our imagination; imagination is a function of both our conscious minds and of our supermind, the all-powerful "Middle Mind" or subconscious.

The consciously controlled use of these remarkable powers is called by many names. I call it *Imaginology*, the controlled channeling of this great mental force to its highest and best use in our lives.

Everything that has happened to us in the past, everything that is happening to us now, or ever will happen to us in the future is the result of our thoughts. *We are what we think we are. We are what we believe ourselves to be.*

As you go through the pages of this book you will understand that *there is no other law* and **why** it must be this way.

Our thoughts are as weak as our fears and as strong as our great expectations. We get out of life what we truly expect to get.

Our thought habits—patterns—the persistent picture of ourselves held in our imaginations, in our conscious minds, determines absolutely the sort of life we will experience from day to day, month to month, year to year. The results are as predictable as the law of gravity that brought the apple down on Sir Isaac Newton's head.

If you harbor persistent fears of poverty and ill health, if you imagine yourself trapped in a morass of want and need, if you feel you are stuck in a rut on the path of progress, if you feel that you are, or may be, the victim of some dreadful disease—then, sooner or later, any or all of these fears will be realized in your life.

But it does not have to be so!

You can change every negative condition in your life. You can do it simply and easily by applying the principles of Imaginology to your day-to-day living. In the following pages you will discover how to do this simply and easily. It will be explained in the clearest language.

The principles of Imaginology are not new. They were first disclosed to us in the Bible. Time and time again, in The Old Testament and in The New Testament, the prophets and, later, Jesus and his disciples repeated the simple formulae.

Down through the ages the greatest teachers and the wisest of men and women have understood and used the principle of Imaginology.

Some have called it concentration. Some have called it meditation. Most frequently, it is referred to as prayer. Whatever the label, what you are doing is *visualizing* something urgently needed in your life and fervently asking that it be materialized.

The exciting part of the principle of Imaginology is this: You can use it alone or on a crowded street, in your car, on a bus, or at thirty-five-thousand feet above the clouds in a speeding jet liner. It makes absolutely no difference.

The only requirement is that you accept the principle and that you believe without a doubt that the power will work for you.

How can you be sure? Read what the enlightened teachers and achievers have said down through the ages.

In John (16:24) Jesus, speaking to his disciples, said, "Ask and ye shall receive that your joy may be full."

Matthew (21:22), understanding the powerful principle, said, "Whatsoever ye shall ask in prayer, believing, ye shall receive."

And Mark (11:24), seeing full well the need for faith all around him, said with the deepest conviction, "What things soever ye desire, when ye pray, believe that ye receive them and ye shall have them."

The operative words are, *Believe and Receive.*

Before you ask for something to be brought into your life, the first thing you must do is visualize clearly what you want.

You must imagine it—imagine not only the condition or thing that you want but you must imagine the pleasure or the relief you will experience when it materializes.

To imagine and to visualize are the same mental acts. The principle of vivid visualization that is the first step to getting the good things you want in life is also the first step in applying the magic of Imaginology to fulfill your desires.

Centuries after those ancient ones whose names have become immortal, many other persons who believed those biblical injunctions and demonstrated that the principle works, shared their knowledge with us.

Napoleon said, "Imagination rules the world." So long as he believed that, *without a doubt,* his armies were victorious. Knowing how the principle of Imaginology works, we can say with equal certainty that he "met his Waterloo" when he allowed doubt to creep in. His mistake in strategy had its roots in some secret uncertainty that undoubtedly was also the ultimate undoing of Hannibal and Alexander the Great.

That is an immutable part of the principle too!

Anatol France whose conquests were in the world of letters, said, "To know is nothing. To imagine is everything."

The great preacher-philosopher, Henry Ward Beecher, said, "The soul without imagination is what an observatory would be without a telescope."

Author Samuel Taylor Coleridge, whose "Rhyme of the Ancient Mariner" is a towering classic of imaginative English literature, wrote, "The primary imagination I hold to be the living power and prime agent of all human perception and a repetition in the finite mind of the eternal act of creation in the infinite I Am."

Joseph Conrad saw it this way: "Only in men's imagination does every truth find an effective and undeniable existence. Imagination, not invention, is the supreme master of art as of life."

Poet Wallace Stevens wrote, "In the world of words the imagination is one of the forces of nature."

John Keats said the same thing in more glowing language.

"I am certain of nothing but the holiness of the heart's affections and the truth of imagination."

Sigmund Freud's one-time student and later founder of a great school of psychology of his own, Carl Gustav Jung, said, "The debt we owe to the play of imagination is incalculable."

Now, having established that enlightened minds down through the centuries have confirmed the principles of visualizing the conditions you want in life and making them materialize through unquestioning belief that the principle works, let's begin to familiarize ourselves with the simple science of Imaginology and what must be done to make it work in your life.

Please remember: it is already working in your life but unless you are consciously using it to bring into your experience those things–good things–that you truly desire, it is running through the sea of your subconscious like a ship without a helmsman.

Don't say, as too many persons do, "Oh gosh, I have no imagination at all!"

You are giving the lie to your statement for you are actually using your imagination negatively. You are simply imagining that you don't have any imagination and by so doing you are proving our point!

Every one of us has the power to imagine.

Every one of us uses the power of imagination every day.

The gift of imagination has been given equally to us all.

Believe that.

It is man's most hopeful prospect.

It is the true key to changing yours into a life of radiant good health, of achievement, and of happiness and plenty.

2

Your Inseparable
Three-Part Self

*You are never alone.
There's far, far more to thee and me
than mortal eyes are wont to see.
Two invisible companions are with you every moment
of every day of your life,
waiting for you to call on them
for advice and help.*

In his first epistle to the Thessalonians, the Apostle Paul wrote, *"I pray God your whole spirit, and soul and body be preserved blameless."*

In that prayer, Paul was recognizing the trilogy of self—the three essential parts that comprise each of us—the spirit, the soul, and the body.

Let's now see how they relate.

How many times have you said, or heard others say, "I can't do it to save my soul"?

Scores of times, probably.

Now why do we say that in precisely that manner?

We say it because we have been taught that our soul is some "divine thing" that exists apart from us, a separate entity that is in danger of being "lost" to us if we do not behave in some prescribed manner, usually dictated by an interpretation of the scriptures according to a particular faith.

Throughout both the Old and the New Testaments there are scores of references to the soul which, if interpreted literally, reinforce the concept of a separate entity related to us, that is at the mercy of our behavior while, at the same time, we are at the mercy of its judgement.

The soul is not a separate entity.
It cannot be taken from us.
We cannot damage it.
It cannot judge us.
It cannot be lost.
It cannot be elevated to heaven or "cast down into the depths of Hell."

Why?

Because, *it is what we are* and *we are it.* All of us, regardless of race, color, or religion, are souls. We are individual expressions of the Universal Soul. We are "poor souls" or "inspired souls" depending upon how we see ourselves—what we really believe ourselves to be.

What we deeply believe ourselves to be, we are.

Repeat: What we deeply believe ourselves to be, we are.

That is the key to the successful use of Imaginology to change yours into a happier, healthier, more abundant life.

It's as simple as that.

Before we go on, let me say something with all due respect to the church—mine—yours—everybody's.

This is not intended to be a "religious book."

It is intended to show that Jesus and all of the great teachers understood and dedicated themselves to telling us that when we were created with the power to reason we were given the power of choice, the opportunity to love or to hate, to build or destroy, the power to live our lives in happiness, love, and abundance, or the power to choose misery, ill health, and want. Every great teacher knew and taught the joy of living a good life to the fullest, of doing our best to achieve the perfection that our Creator had in mind for us when we were brought forth on this earth.

That is what Imaginology is all about.

It does not ask you to believe anything contrary to those teachings that comfort you the most.

It *does* ask you to believe that you are not at the mercy of anything but your own deeply held convictions about what you are.

Again: You are what you deeply believe yourself to be.

Nobody can change that but you.

In Proverbs we are assured that "as a man thinketh, so is he."

Time after time we are told that simple truth. How then does such a miracle happen? What part, if any, does our soul play in it?

The soul's function has been explained countless times and in many ways. The explanation has often been obscured by those who believe that anything even remotely "religious" that can be explained in simple terms cannot possibly be of any real value.

Not true!

How much simpler can the working of the universal principle be explained than in the promises of Matthew and Mark and in the scores of reassurances given us by Jesus Himself?

For clarity, then, let us call the soul by a simpler name.

Let us call it, *Subconscious Mind.*

Our subconscious mind is the second or middle part of our inseparable three-part selves.

First comes the Universal Spirit, The Creator, The All There Is, The Great I Am, or in a far more familiar term, simply God, the source of all there is, of all there ever has been or will be.

Second comes the soul, our subconscious mind.

Third comes the conscious mind, our thinking self, the consciously thinking, imagining mind that operates through the brain, the mind that lets you read these words and understand the beautiful simplicity of your being.

"As a man thinketh, so is he."

It's all there—in just seven words.

In contemporary language it can be said like this:

You are what you deeply believe yourself to be.

You were what you deeply believed yourself to have been.

You will become what you deeply believe you will be.

How long do we have to be sold on the simple truth?

If, to fill a sermon (or a book!), teachers and preachers and scribes seem to wrap that simple kernel of truth in an outer husk of verbiage that really says the same thing in a more complicated way, it is because they are aware that it is no easy matter for most of us to accept the simple truth.

In the order of creation we said the soul—the subconscious mind—is the centerpiece of the Trinity of Being. That order is from the perspective of the source of all creation.

From man's perspective the trinity looks like this:

Your Conscious Mind.
Your Subconscious Mind.
The Infinite Mind or the Source of All Being.

All one must remember is the simple relationship of those parts of yourself—those three inseparable parts that comprise all that you are.

Now, let's go about seeing how the conscious mind, the subconscious mind, and the Infinite Mind relate and work together when you call upon them to create in your present life those good things that you deeply believe you want and need.

3

How Each Part of Your Being Relates

*Infinite mind and your subconscious mind
are inseparable parts of your being.
When you recognize them
as such nothing you ask for
will be denied.*

Once again, *the practice of Imaginology is the "soul" of simplicity.*

Your conscious mind initiates a thought.

Your subconscious mind accepts it.

The Infinite Mind, responding to the subconscious, provides all that it needs to materialize the thought.

How much is materialized depends on how devoutly you believe.

"As a man thinketh . . . " (As he deeply believes)

" . . . believing, ye shall receive . . . "

" . . . when ye pray, believe that ye shall receive . . . "

Belief, then, is the *mental motive power* that transforms your thoughts into material fact.

Once more:

Your conscious mind initiates a thought. It must be a clear and distinct thought.

Your subconscious mind "hears it" and begins to implement it—to make it happen.

Infinite Mind—some call it Super Mind—that knows everything and creates everything, provides your subconscious mind with all that it needs to materialize your thought. It does so in direct proportion to the depth of your belief.

Get those three simple steps firmly in your mind. They are valid. They always work.

If you stop and review your life to the present you must reach the only sensible conclusion. You are where you put yourself. You put yourself there by the positive or negative use of your conscious mind.

Don't blame it on good luck or bad luck. They are both entirely within your conscious control. Blessings don't "just happen." Neither do accidents. We program our subconscious to make them happen.

A friend of mine who made an overnight ascent to stardom when he sang the romantic lead in a hit Broadway musical saw himself as a star and used his native talent to attain his goal.

One night at Sardi's after his performance he confided to me that he had been suffering from an ongoing nightmare. Each night, well past midnight, he drove home to New Jersey.

"I don't know why this thing bugs me," he said with a deeply troubled expression, "but I can't seem to shake the vision of a head-on crash. I've never had a bad accident, but for some damned reason I keep imagining this one—and I can't see beyond it!"

A few weeks later my telephone rang in the middle of the night. "Your friend, Don, was killed tonight in a head-on crash on the turnpike. They think he went to sleep at the wheel."

Thus ended the promising career of Don Richards, a brilliant young performer who seemed to have sensed his own tragic end. Call it intuition, precognition, or whatever. A psychologist might say that Don mistrusted his sudden rise to stardom, even though he had consciously done all of the things necessary to deserve it. He believed he could get there, but perhaps he did not believe that he could stay there.

Or, he may have been penalizing himself, for some closely guarded personal reason that not even those closest to him suspected. We shall never know.

How many times since then have I wished that I had consciously understood the principle of Imaginology so that I might have helped Don understand himself. I had been making the principle I call Imaginology work successfully in my own life for years!

Another, happier example stems from my own show business days in New York.

One of the pioneer television shows in the pre-network days was *The Swift Show*, a half-hour musical on NBC-TV, starring the widely loved tenor singing lead of the hit radio show, *Show Boat*. Who among us who remembers those days can forget Lanny Ross and his familiar theme song, "Moonlight and Roses"?

Each week with Lanny we looked for an outstanding young talent to introduce. (Don Richards had been one of them.)

One day a talent agent came to my office with a very beautiful young soprano from Wenatchee, Washington. Her name was Martha Wright.

I listened to her demonstration record and was impressed. She had a glorious and true voice. We signed her for one guest appearance at a very modest $100.

She made such a hit that we signed her as a "regular" until a Broadway producer heard her and made her an offer she could not refuse.

Martha Wright became a true Broadway musical star when she replaced Mary Martin in the leading role in *South Pacific*!

Martha made that dream come true. Later she made another one come true. At the peak of her stardom she met the man she could really fall deeply in love with.

Despite pleas to remain in the musical theater, Martha married happily and set about making another dream come true, to have a loving husband and a family of her own.

There is still another happy ending to a long-held dream. This involves two people, a former band leader turned talent manager and a young singing star from Oklahoma.

Jack Rael stopped me one day in the hall outside the studio at 30 Rockefeller Plaza, the home of NBC Radio and its pioneer television operation. It was the fall of 1948.

"Lee," he said, "I would like you to listen to a young singer I've been working with back in Oklahoma. She's had her own radio show there for a dairy. She's really been racking up the ratings."

I knew Jack as a thoroughgoing professional who was given to understatement. I arranged to hear an audition, was thoroughly impressed, and signed the young lady for a guest shot on *The Swift Show.*

The young lady's name? Patti Page.

As I recall, our budget in those days was $100 for the show, which included a solo and a duet with Lanny Ross.

In 1957, as the producer of *The Big Record* on CBS-TV for Oldsmobile, we paid Patti $7,500 as the star of her own show.

As this is being written, Patti and Jack Rael, her manager for more than thirty years, are packing to go to Japan for a series of appearances.

Their mutual dream came true—the star and the manager—because neither of them ever stopped believing it would!

In all my years as a writer-producer-director in show business I never saw an enduring success, either on stage or off, that was not a perfect illustration of the power of Imaginology—the power of belief in the miracles that can be effected by our subconscious mind. And I've worked a few of those "miracles" myself, for which I am eternally grateful!

The urge to make it on our own begins very early in life. So does the conviction that we can.

Ever since childhood when you first became capable of concepts of yourself and your relation to the exciting new world you were beginning to explore—when your thoughts first began to move outward from those elemental dependence desires to be fed, sheltered, loved, and made secure—you began to experience a sense of self that said, "One day I will leave the protection of family and home and be a free-standing, free-willed individual."

How many times did we say, "I can hardly wait until I grow up?"

How many times have we heard our impatient young people say that?

The urge to express ourselves as individuals must have been voiced somehow in the grunts of primitive man. The first coming-of-age ceremonies, and much later the confirmation rituals acknowledging individual responsibility, such as the Jewish Bar Mitzvah and numberless other modern confirmation rituals, are all evidence of our inner desire to stand alone and make our way as individuals.

Another commonly asked question—one asked by adults of young people—is, "What do you want to be when you grow up?"

We can find convincing evidence of the creative process at work within the bosoms of our own families.

At fourteen my stepson, Michael, told me that he wanted to be a fireman or a soccer player. Those two possibilities intrigued him for understandable reasons. Inherent in both professions is individual recognition within a group that receives wide public attention.

Now twenty, on a baseball scholarship at the University of Texas, Mike is on his way to becoming a promising young pitcher with great natural skill. Abetted by his superb physique, this six-foot-seven young giant can wind up and release a formidable variety of pitches, some of which travel across the plate at close to ninety miles an hour!

The scouts are looking. If Mike continues to believe deeply and work with his present dedication, it is a foregone conclusion that he will be scouted and taken to a league farm team.

It would not surprise any of us who know and admire him to turn on the TV set some day and hear "Vin" Scully announce, "the starting pitcher will be Mike Dunn."

His seventeen-year-old sister, Elizabeth, had no such early indecision about a career. From the time she entered ballet pre-school in Israel, where business kept her family for two-and-a-half years, until she entered ballet school in Belgium, Lisa had only one ambition, to be a prima ballerina.

Ballet was to be her life. She has pursued her training in Europe and in the United States with such single-minded devotion that this lovely young lady has been given a full scholarship with the renowned San Francisco Ballet School.

One of five students to be chosen for the tour, "Lisa" has just returned from five weeks in Italy, Sicily, Israel, Greece, and a week in Chicago at the Ravinia Festival. A Hawaiian tour is next!

Both of these young people are using the principle of Imaginology and they are proving it works.

If you are tempted to say, "Yes, but like the others you've talked about, they have special talents," don't do it. It is not true. We all have *some* special talent for creative expression, from Russian John and his scrimshaw work, to architect Frank Lloyd Wright, whose transcendental talent for harmonizing man's abode with nature expanded his art into whole new frontiers.

To know that you have the ability to envision your ultimate goal, the faith to believe in your ability to attain it, and the joyful willingness to do everything possible to prepare for its realization—*that is the secret!*

> Envision your goal.
> Believe in your ability to attain it.
> Be willing to work to reach it.

Do not wait for fate to serve life up to you on a silver platter. You've got to meet your subconscious at least halfway when you ask it to materialize your wishes. The more willing you are to dedicate yourself to your end of the bargain, the more willing the subconscious is to see that you attain it.

> *Your conscious mind* speaks with authority and conviction.
>
> *Your subconscious mind* listens and acts. It never questions the wisdom of your request, for it knows that is a function, a responsibility, of the conscious mind.
>
> *The Infinite Mind* supplies everything necessary for the subconscious mind to bring into your life those things you *deeply believe* you want.

The process never fails.

Believe that! Remember, that same process operates to create the conditions you are experiencing today, no matter what those circumstances may be.

If you would change those circumstances, if you would improve your health, your financial position, your social position, anything—or any condition in your life—then you must envision—*imagine*—clearly what you want and believe without question that such good things will be materialized in your life experience here, through the operation of your subconscious mind. Others have them. Why not you?

I call my subconscious mind, "My good friend, S. C." It is not likely that you will treat a good friend inconsiderately. You have no more willing and loyal friend. S. C. is totally unselfish. It deserves to be treated with all of the consideration possible. It will respond in kind.

4

How Imaginology
Works

*You use your imagination
constantly. Thinking is "inner talking."
So mind what you "say
to yourself";
your subconscious mind never wanders;
it always pays attention. It is
always ready to make happen
in your life those things,
positive and negative,
that you are imagining.*

From our point of perception the Universal Mind or the Infinite Spirit is greater than the sum of its parts. It is the whole of our universe and of all the other universes that scientists are now certain exist.

In its abstract sense its full nature is beyond our present comprehension. We may theorize endlessly about the nature of The All There Is, as Seth, "a personality from another world," defines Infinite Spirit in his remarkable communications transmitted through trance medium-author, Jane Roberts, assisted by her artist husband, Robert Butts.

Robert has transcribed hundreds of thousands of words that have been spoken by Seth through Jane. These communications have opened breathtaking vistas of the universal nature of life, vistas that have dumbfounded even the most skeptical readers of the many Seth books.

Communications from "a personality from another world" imply a hereafter or at least a "heretofore." Implicit also in the communications is the possibility of a continuation of our spirit-selves through reincarnation.

It is possible to discuss the theory of reincarnation for days and nights without end and present seemingly endless piles of evidence from reputable people—scientists, philosophers, and religionists alike—and it is highly unlikely that the aetheist or the dyed-in-the-wool skeptic will be convinced. It is the God-given right of these people to believe as they will. No person as such has ever changed another person's beliefs. But the *reason* communicated in his or her words may. Since eons before The Inquisition, many a zealot has forfeited life rather than adopt the ideas of another, whether, in the long run, that person is right or wrong.

It is not the purpose of Imaginology to "convert" anybody. Its only purpose is to set forth as clearly as possible a universal law that has been revealed, without exception, by the great teachers whose insight and belief have changed the world. Anyone is free to believe in the validity of the law—or not to believe. A lot of people contend that they do not believe even while they are demonstrating its effectiveness every day of their lives. If they don't believe, they believe they don't! It makes no difference to the operation of the subconscious. It doesn't even know the meaning of "ego trip."

It is not important whether or not the evidence so far in support of the theory of life after death and life before death convinces a person of the continuation of life, or whether he or she believes that the promise of a hereafter—of reincarnation— simply speaks to and palliates our secret fears that physical death is the end of us, that the promise of an afterlife is nothing more than a cruel joke.

But perpetrated by whom?

The ultimate cynic said, "If there were no God man would have to invent one."

Really?

If there were no God, who invented the cynic?

Quite apart from the promise in the Bible, "In my father's house are many mansions," (John 14:2) there is a growing body of evidence, from Edgar Cacey, Betty White, Elizabeth Kübler-Ross, Ruth Montgomery, Jeane Dixon, Dr. Moody, and, most convincingly, from Seth himself, that this life of ours is not the be-all, end-all of our existence—that we are indeed far more than meets the mortal eye.

Were it not so, none of us would ever know the joy of achieving our cherished dreams. Who among us—who has dared to dream and to do—would argue that we are no more than a "rag and a bone and a hank of hair," as Kipling wrote in "The Vampire"?

Dreams do not come true because there is a Celestial Scoreboard on which is logged our progress and our worthiness to succeed. Neither does Saint Peter sit by The Pearly Gates checking our report cards to determine our fitness to graduate into The Kingdom of Heaven.

We alone determine the directions our lives take.

Ella Wheeler Wilcox stated this truth most eloquently in her perceptive poem, "The Winds of Fate."

> At the turn of the present century poetess Ella Wheeler Wilcox likened our lives to sailing ships at sea. One ship may be driving to the east and another to the west, but neither ship is at the mercy of the "gale," for it is how their captains have ordered the sails set that determines the direction in which they go.

It is the set of our minds, then, and not the whim of some fate beyond our control that "tells us the way to go."

Determining the set of our minds is the entire purpose of the simple science of Imaginology. We do not have to suffer "the slings and arrows of outrageous fortune" as poor Hamlet feared. The choice is ours. The course we chart through life is determined by the set of our minds. Do we set sail before a favorable wind or do we find ourselves "in irons" on a dangerous lee shore?

It is up to us.

When William Henley wrote in *Invictus*, "*I am the master of my fate, I am the captain of my soul,*" he echoed the promise of Jesus and all of the other great teachers who preceded and followed Him that we alone determine the quality of the lives we live on earth.

It must be clear then that if we would change our lives for the better, we must change our beliefs about ourselves. It is all well and good to say that such a mental turnaround is a simple thing to accomplish.

In essence, it is. But we are creatures of habit and one of the most pernicious habits is negative thinking. "Try making a habit of it," we were counselled about saying our prayers or brushing our teeth or folding our clothes.

Good actions can become habitual too. Our purpose in these pages is to convince you that you should become "hooked" on positive thinking about yourselves and all of the conditions that surround you.

Those who are weighed down with habitual negative thoughts and see all around them the unhappy manifestations of such thinking without ever realizing that their lives reflect their beliefs, good or bad, are trapped.

They are trapped for the very reason that they believe their troubles are the result of some unjust fate that has singled them our for poverty, ill health, marital discord, and other unhappiness.

Nothing could be further from the truth!

In the next five to ten minutes you can prove to yourself that your thoughts determine how you feel and, if held long enough and believed in devoutly enough, will also dictate what happens in your life.

Try it—now. Mark this page and put the book aside for a few minutes.

Then, get comfortable.

Close your eyes.

Next—and don't be shocked by this suggestion—recall as vividly as possible one of the saddest or most troublesome events in your recent life, something you remember clearly.

Recall it—visualize it—in as much detail as you can. Recall all of the circumstances surrounding it. Let yourself feel the painful emotions that attended the event. Do it deliberately until you have made yourself thoroughly unhappy.

All right, you've done it.

What has happened?

By recalling in detail all the events that surrounded your unhappiness you have made yourself miserable all over again! You are experiencing all of the trauma—the pain of the injury—that resulted.

Now then, let's turn your head around. Turn your thoughts to the happiest thing that ever happened to you thus far. Remember it in all of its rich and pleasant detail. Really concentrate on remembering, on imagining that it is all happening to you again—right now—this minute.

Feel all the emotion you felt at the time—the joy, the satisfaction, the sense of accomplishment, the freedom from trouble, the elation—every positive and pleasant emotion.

Again, you must use your imagination to re-create the condition. Lose yourself in the happy recollection. See the people who shared the event with you. Hear their congratulations—the good and positive things they said that reinforced your faith in yourself. You were a winner then. Not a loser.

All right now, you've done that too.

What has happened this time?

Recalling the experience produced a great happiness in you. No question about that! But something else has happened now, too.

You have proved something to yourself. You have proved that it is no longer necessary to question further the effect your conscious mind can have on your physical body. Those effects are emotions. Emotions always follow thoughts.

Many people say, "I'm at the mercy of my emotions." Nonsense! You are at the mercy of your thoughts."

So, having demonstrated to yourself that you can produce both positive and negative effects simply by turning your mind, by imagining happy and unhappy events in your life, should it really be so difficult to understand how your deeply held beliefs about the past, the present, and the future can affect you?

The same imagination that produced two opposite results when you thought of two different past events can be used to visualize the good and happy things that you need to insure a happy and fruitful life in the immediate future.

The principle that caused both effects is the same. The same flame that warms you can consume you. It depends entirely upon how it is used. As you sit reading this, no matter what your circumstances or condition, your thoughts and your belief in them made the sort of personal world you presently inhabit.

No arbitrary fate sentenced you to unhappiness.

No arbitrary fate sentenced you to ill health.

No arbitrary fate sentenced you to poverty.

No arbitrary fate sentenced you to loneliness and fear.

No arbitrary fate prevents you from achieving everything you need.

If all these things seem unattainable now, it is because, by your thoughts alone, you have made them so.

Think of the good things you have already achieved—little things. How did you get them? You believed you could get them and you did everything that was necessary to do so.

Your subconscious doesn't give a "tinker's damn" about size. It delivers what you requisition. Quantity and size are not a condition. Their only limitation is that which you put on them.

In this chapter, How Imaginology Works, I have emphasized the operating principle behind this simple science of mind control.

Since I firmly believe that nobody has a right to try to teach something solely from academic theory, let me give you the first of several practical examples of Imaginology at work, examples directly out of my own experience.

When my daughter, Allison, was two and a half years old she used to ride down the Toll Road on Vermont's famous Mount Mansfield near the village of Stowe on the front of my unwieldy old Attenhoffer skis, then the latest thing in equipment.

She was a precious little cargo so I was a bit uptight and very careful. I can still see her excited little face framed in the fur trim of her parka hood peering up at me and crying gleefully, "Faster, Daddy! Faster!" Fear had no meaning for her.

For some years now Allison, an expert skier, has been working for the Skiing Corporation in Aspen, Colorado. She has her own three-year-old now, my granddaughter, Gwendolyn.

This past winter, after surprisingly little instruction from her mother, Gwennie began skiing all by herself on Snowmass's famous Fanny Hill.

After not having skied for thirty years I went back to it at my daughter's urging.

"It's like riding a bike, Dad," she reassured me. "You never forget how."

She was right. I had not forgotten the basic principles of handling skis as I had learned them back in the early 1940s.

Some things had not changed—the snowplow and the snowplow turn, for example. But other things had. Parallel skiing had all but made obsolete a lot of the old Stem Christies and other power turns, maneuvers that required a lot of upper-body torque to get the skis to change direction without putting excessive strain on the old soft boots and the dangerous "bear trap" bindings that made the local bone setter the most affluent citizen in town!

Even though I knew better, I approached this refound adventure with two negatives: I was afraid I was too old now to tackle the mountain, and I mistrusted the complicated looking new equipment that appeared to me like something out of Buck Rogers' closet.

I got fitted with rental equipment; I certainly was not going to blow 500 bucks on the latest gear, only to find that my fears were well founded and, finally, I set out for the bottom of the lift.

No hog on ice moved more gingerly than I. After a near disaster while catching the chair lift from behind with a handful of ski poles I managed to get to the top of the first slope.

Fanny Hill, aptly named, is a beginners' slope. To me it looked perpendicular. Going over Niagara Falls in a barrel suddenly seemed simpler and safer. Even so, the slope was filled with pint-sized, absolutely fearless little snow bunnies schussing their way back down to the lift. The slope was also dotted with taut-muscled beginners whose terrified eyes shone saucer-round through their tinted spacemen's goggles.

Finally, after stalling as long as self-respect would permit, I took a deep breath and started down the slope. Echoing through those long past decades were the words of the Austrian skimaster who had taught me the basics.

Following his explicit instructions, I got my shoulders and arms into position and drove my upper body, all 190 pounds of it, into the turn.

Three seconds later I lay in a jackstraw heap of skis and poles, having executed a completely out-of-control 360-degree turn!

As I looked up sheepishly, goggles askew, I saw my daughter's smile. Because I knew her so well, I was certain it was intended to be sympathetic.

"Gee, Dad," she said as she bent to help me up, "I meant to tell you that the whole principle of control is much simpler now with these new G. L. M. skis, and safety bindings, and the new, high, plastic boots."

Dale Carnegie would have been enormously proud of her tact.

" You don't have to use your upper body anymore," she continued. "It's all done with your feet."

Two days later, after some pointers from her, I was enjoying skiing with Allison more than I ever imagined I could as we shared the beauty of the high slopes while traversing the upper reaches of Snowmass and Buttermilk.

The moral of the story?

It all depends on your mental approach.

Most of us, from the time we are small children, are being brainwashed with negatives that are intended to protect us.

The "don't-do-this, don't-do-that" edicts begin to inculcate our subconscious minds with a series of prohibitions designed to ward off dangers, physical and moral. In the end those very warnings make us the victims of the dangers.

Seth, through the remarkable writer-medium, Jane Roberts, in a discussion of the negative processes that attract to us the very things we fear, used as an example a family in an affluent neighborhood whose house was repeatedly robbed while other, equally tempting targets were left untouched.

The reason was simple. The family members lived in constant fear and expectation that they would be robbed. Their conscious fear-thoughts impregnated the universal subconscious with that mental picture. In turn, it was transmitted to the criminal minds who prey on such people.

The family expected to be robbed—*believed it would be*—and it was!

Again—good or bad—positive or negative—*your thoughts are as powerful as your expectations.*

The negative conditioning that begins with well-intentioned parents in childhood—and mind you, some of those common sense warnings are necessary—is continued into adulthood. If anything, it is increased.

Think for a moment about the barrage of negative advertising that we are subjected to every time we turn on the radio or the television set and, very often, as we thumb through our newspapers and periodicals.

The insurance companies comprise a huge ministry of fear—fear of premature death, fear of serious illness, fear of fire and theft, fear of accidents and liabilities of every description.

The drug manufacturers comprise another huge ministry of fear—fear of a score of ailments from which "seven out of ten" people suffer. Such misery, they imply, can best be relieved by using their pills, ointments, syrups, pastilles, capsules, and sprays. Some of them work because we believe they do.

Even the dedicated scientists at the Food and Drug Administration comprise a subliminal ministry of fear in their efforts to protect us against questionable nostrums, contaminants in food and drink, and many of our pleasures, including the use of tobacco and sugar substitutes.

After awhile one must reach the conclusion that it is indeed "a blankety-blank jungle out there," to paraphrase with discretion an old Tarzan joke. One inescapable fact dawns on us at last. Living may be hazardous to our health!

Again, this is not to imply that common sense precautions are not wise. But in those instances where we are deliberately conditioned, subliminally or otherwise, to fear something in order to induce us to buy a product, we are being inexorably propelled toward a sort of free-floating anxiety that can fasten itself on almost any human condition.

We find ourselves living in fear that bad things will happen to us. Paradoxically, we are afraid that good things will not happen to us.

The simple fact is—everything that happens to us is the result of our ingrained convictions. Nothing is preordained by fate. There is nothing in our lives that cannot be changed for the better by consciously impressing our subconscious mind with deeply held positive beliefs—vividly conceived mental images of the good things we wish to materialize in our lives.

When I was discussing Imaginology with a young minister friend shortly before this book was begun, the pastor of a flock of sincerely seeking young married couples suddenly frowned and said, "You've just turned me on to something."

He laughed quietly. "You know, a lot of my couples have asked that I delete the word 'obey' from the wedding ceremony. Since I understand how they feel in this day of the equality of the sexes, I'm happy to do it."

He shook his head and smiled again. "It has just occurred to me, though, that elsewhere in the ceremony there are at least two negatives that might well be deleted. I'm thinking about 'for better or for worse' and 'in sickness and in health.'"

The young minister got up and stood looking out of the window for a time. Then he turned. "If I understand you correctly, we are, in all innocence, preconditioning our young couples to . . . to . . . I suppose the word is 'expect' the worst with the better and the sickness with the health."

He returned to his seat, frowning. "I'll be sticking my clerical neck out, but I'm going to call a group of my young parishioners together and try it out on them. I'm going to suggest some new wording that turns their thoughts toward a full and rich life—that emphasizes the positive by ignoring the negative—that turns them toward the deep anticipation of the rich and vital life that must come from sincerely said prayers.

"I recall a passage in Job that is confirmed time and time again in The New Testament: 'Thou shalt also decree a thing, and it shall be established unto thee; and the light shall shine upon thy ways.'

"Someday," he continued, "I believe I'll go through the testaments and search out those positive promises. I'm beginning to see that what you are doing is reiterating, in contemporary language, what may be the most often voiced promise in the scriptures. If I am right, that alone could inspire some of the most meaningful sermons I could preach."

Some weeks later, when I saw him again, he went out of his way to say that he was right about the promises. The injunction to believe with all one's heart is expressed scores of time in the Bible and in as many different ways.

The act of believing is fundamental to the effective practice, not only of the Christian faith but of all others as well.

So, to be forewarned about the subjective, mind-bending effect of much of our advertising and the negative aspect of much of our news is to be forearmed.

Later, in the final pages of this book, we will suggest how the mass practice of Imaginology could, if we were to erase all of the alleged divisions between people and nations, change the "shape of the earth" more surely than all of our atom bombs.

5

How to Make Imaginology Work for You

*Your "other two selves"
are always on the job ready to help
you make a happy, healthy,
fulfilling life.*

Few people doubt the assertion, "You are what you eat." They can visualize the positive effect on the body of good nutrition and the negative effect of a poor diet. At one time or another most of us have felt these effects in our own bodies.

Why then, should it be any less easy to accept the assertion, "You are what you think?"

Far more often than you realize you feel the positive effect of good thoughts in your life. You also feel the negative effects when you allow thoughts of illness, want, and unhappiness to dominate your thinking.

You know you can change the effect of poor eating habits on your body simply by changing your diet. *Just as simply, you can change the effect of negative thoughts on your life by changing the way you think.*

In the foregoing pages we have shown how Imaginology works. We have shown that what happens to us day by day depends entirely on how we use the miraculous gift of imagination.

Now, let us see how Imaginology can work for you.

Just as the principles of psychology can be perverted to brainwash a person for evil ends or to redirect personal action into positive channels, so can the principle of Imaginology be used both positively and negatively.

That is what is meant when we say, "You are what you think," or, more precisely, *"You are what you believe yourself to be."*

You have demonstrated for yourself the effect that unhappy and happy recollections can have on you by trying the exercise in Chapter 4. In a sense it was just a "free trial sample" of the reactions that can be induced by using your imagination. What you felt was determined by what you thought. You had a choice. You made it. The result was predictable and automatic.

Given the freedom of choice, then, who would deliberately choose to cling to negative thoughts that can only produce negative results when simply by choosing to change to positive thoughts it is possible to bring into fruition all of the good things necessary for a happy, healthy, fully expressed and secure life?

How many times have you heard someone say, "Nobody in his right mind would do a thing like that"?

Such a statement is usually made when a person has done something exceedingly foolish. Perhaps it will not be amiss to say that any of us, understanding now that by changing our thinking we can change our lives for the better, would certainly not be "in our right minds"—would be foolish in the extreme—if we refused or failed to take advantage of the miraculous power that lies in the positive partnership of our conscious and subconscious minds.

So, let's resolve not to ignore this great potential blessing and get down to the business of learning how to use the God-given power that has been given equally to us all.

First, make a priority list of the good things you want to bring into your life. Put them down in the order of their priority—of their importance to you.

Do not make the list too long. If it turns out to be a veritable "laundry list" of things you need, quite possibly you'll look at it, grow discouraged, and be tempted to say, "How can I possibly bring about all these things into my life?"

If you try to get it all at once you will confuse your great silent partner, the subconscious mind. Take no more than three objectives at the most. Two is better. One is best! After you have visualized your first priority clearly for a time, release it with a request to your friend, the subconscious, to act on it in its own time.

Do not set deadlines.

Do not tell your subconscious how to do its job.

It will help you to visualize what you want clearly if you'll imagine your conscious mind is being focused down like a burning glass, or a big spotlight. See it shining brightly on the image or condition that you wish to materialize. See it clearly in your "mind's eye." If your mind starts to stray, bring it back. Keep it on a mental leash. Do not worry if it tends to wander a bit. It happens to us all until we learn to discipline our thoughts.

There are several good techniques you can use to warm up your powers of concentration.

One I use successfully is to imagine I'm driving down the main street of my town. Mentally, I see the cross streets. In the beginning I had to settle for just the principal streets with traffic lights. Soon, however, I could name most of the streets for a two-mile stretch. For those I needed help on I memorized one or more of the principal buildings occupying the corner. It worked very well.

Another good technique is to start at one hundred and count backward down to zero. *Be sure to count backward.* That will make you concentrate. Either of those exercises are simply warm-ups to get you focused on one objective for a period of time.

What you are doing is taking the first "baby step" on an exciting journey to a rich new life.

You are doing what we all have done when we learned to drive a car. You are sitting behind the wheel familiarizing yourself with the controls and the instruments before you begin actually to drive.

Two or three times a day practice visualizing what you want in as much detail as you can imagine. Soon you will find that the imaginary pictures come more easily and clearly. Keep at it. Do it for two or three days.

You are not really materializing what you want yet, but you are taking the first all-important step. You are "seeing" it.

The second step is to *feel* it. This means to feel it *emotionally.*

If what you are concentrating on is a new home, visualize your ideal house in an ideal location. In your mind's eye see it complete with all the features you desire to make you and your loved ones happy and comfortable.

It will help you to visualize it and send a more vivid picture to your subconscious mind where the magic of Imaginology actually happens, if you imagine yourself walking up to the front door, reaching out for the gleaming brass handle, touching it, opening the door, stepping into the entryway, and pausing to look around.

Feel the tile or the slate or the rich pile of the carpet under your feet. Feel the spaciousness of the rooms as you explore them. See them as you wish them to be.

When you step outside into the yard feel the lawn underfoot. See the gardens. Smell the clean, fresh air and the perfume of the blossoms. See and feel everything you wish to have in and around your ideal home.

React to your emotions. Feel them. Feel deeply the reality of your surroundings. Do not doubt that they exist.

What you are doing, to use our driving analogy again, is turning the key in the ignition to start the motor. You are doing it by seeing and feeling the reality of your ideal home.

Very soon you will find that it is getting much easier to visualize what you want. You will find that it is much easier to "get the feel" of your dream. It won't be necessary then to spend several days exercising your mind before you set it to the task of directing your subconscious to materialize the good things you want. You can do it immediately. To pursue our analogy, you are ready to put your dream into gear and head out on the highway to realization.

The third step—the one that is critical if you would make your vision come true—is to BELIEVE. *Believe that what you want already exists.*

Don't be tempted by skepticism. Don't be tempted to say, "What do you mean, 'It already exists'? So far the whole thing is just a figment of my imagination!"

What is it the kids say? "Oh, yeah? That shows just how much *you* know about it!"

Until you get used to the nature and the operation of the principle of Imaginology, you might very well echo those words. But consider this for a moment: If you look around you, I defy you to find one single object that did not first have an idea, a concept, behind it.

It might have been a working drawing, a blue print, a rough sketch, or maybe just a clear vision of the thing to be made in the mind of the maker.

That goes for every material thing you can imagine on this earth from the first primitive utensils and weapons to the most sophisticated satellite that can tell you the color of a man's eyes from twenty-five-thousand miles out in space.

Nothing exists—not even man himself—that did not first have a plan, a vision, a blueprint, a concept of some sort that preceded the creation in material form.

What you are doing with your visualization and your believing is registering your "blueprint" with your subconscious mind. It then becomes the prime contractor who is to create what you visualized. *What binds the contract is your belief. Your belief guarantees its delivery!*

Above all, remember this: *You are not pretending. You are not playacting.* You are not "daydreaming" about impossible things. Realistically speaking there are no "impossible dreams."

Unless you desert the world of reality like some poor souls do in an effort to escape and imagine yourself to be the King of England or Napoleon or some other majestic character, there are no impossible dreams. Good health is possible. Wealth is possible. A wonderful mate and family are possible. A congenial job is possible. The development of a rewarding talent is possible. Look around you at those who are enjoying such blessings. Of course they're possible. And in these pages you are learning how to make them possible in your life, if you do not already have some or all of them.

Imaginology is not a "new science." It is simply an easy-to-remember, accurate label for the ancient process for managing our minds that was handed down through the ages by the great teachers who have understood the miraculously simple working of the Eternal Creative Principle.

What did Mark (11:24) say? "What things soever ye desire when ye pray, believe that ye receive them and ye shall have them."

And Matthew (21:22)? "Whatsoever ye shall ask in prayer, believing, ye shall receive."

Each time the operative word is the same: *Believe!*

To imagine is to create a mental image of something you wish. To visualize something you wish is exactly the same thing.

Those "things soever that ye desire . . ." are the things you see in your mind's eye—the things you imagine—visualize.

They are the good things you pray for.

When you ask for those things in a state of true believing, and you see them as already existing, you set in motion an immutable law that will materialize them according to the power of your belief.

How simple the process! How easy to remember!

To make sure you remember the steps, I have devised a method that makes use of the universally known trade name of a great electronics industrial complex, I.B.M.

I. stands for Imagine
B. stands for Believe
M. stands for Materialize.

Come to think of it, it is the same principle that T. J. Watson used to create his remarkable International Business Machine corporation.

He visualized his great electronics complex. He believed in his vision. He saw it as already existing and he was guided to make the right decisions that were necessary to materialize it.

Whether consciously used or not, the founders of all great enterprises used the basic principles of Imaginology to materialize their dreams.

The process does not work exclusively for special people. *It works for everybody.*

If you find it easier to imagine or visualize what you want by using a device, here is one that works very well for most people. Since it makes use of familiar equipment, you will have no trouble with the basic visualization.

Imagine a home movie screen like the ones most of us use with our projectors. (Imagine a TV screen if you'd rather.)

Set up your mental screen, then relax and view the image you desire. See it projected on your imaginary screen in all of its vivid detail.

After a few minutes imagine yourself moving in closer for a better look. Move in until the frame of the screen disappears from view and you see only the image you have projected.

Continue the process. See it. Feel it—and *Believe* that your vision exists as a reality now.

Then, knowing that you have set the principle in motion, release it. Don't work hard at imagining. Relax. Summon the mental pictures easily. The subconscious mind apparently does not like to be forced or coerced into doing something any more than any of us consciously do.

Don't say that something has to happen at exactly 9:27 in the morning. Don't restrict the process by imposing limitations on it. Just believe it will happen.

It will.

One of the outstanding examples of the power of Imaginology is Florida's Representative Claude Pepper.

At 82 he is beginning to realize another of his many dreams—to step up to the chairmanship of the powerful House Rules Committee in order to pursue his fight to demand that older Americans are valued at their true worth in our society.

On a campaign trip to California not long ago he looked the television cameras of the three major networks and a half dozen independent stations right in the eye and said with the conviction of a man who knows whereof he speaks, "Don't be afraid to dream. Don't be afraid to dare!"

Everyone who has ever dreamed but doubted secretly that dreams can be made to happen should adopt Claude Pepper's words as a personal credo. To paraphrase this remarkable man's inspiring example of the power of faith (*believing!*) we could say, "Don't be afraid to dream—*at any age*. Don't be afraid to believe that dreams do come true!"

When we let doubt creep into our minds to cast shadows over our dreams and aspirations we are literally *driving through life with one foot on the brake.*

There is not a person who does not experience uncertainty about something at some time.

If that uncertainty concerns your present place in life, if you are not sure that you are in your right place, that your job is really the right one for you, that in it you cannot express yourself fully—or, if you are presently out of work and are looking for the right situation, your belief in the power of the subconscious, by way of the conscious use of Imaginology, can lead you—*guide* you is a better word—to the best possible situation for your growth.

To be led implies a move with little or no volition of your own. To be guided implies a willingness to respond to valued suggestions—to move of our own volition. The ways are shown to us but it is up to us to take advantage of them.

This is done by programming our mental computers with positive images of our objectives and pushing the "On" switch to power our subconscious with belief.

One way to do that is to sit down, relax and say:

> *My subconscious mind knows everything about me. It knows all of the talents and skills I possess. Consciously now, I ask my subconscious mind to make known to me the path I should choose to bring to me and mine the greatest happiness and security in life.*
>
> *I believe with absolute faith in the power of the subconscious and in its ability to reveal to me the right decisions and to bring into my life the people and the circumstances that will make my growth possible.*

Don't merely repeat the words by rote without really thinking what they mean. Feel the power implied in them, for what you are really doing is praying in contemporary language.

Never mind that you are not using the *thees* and *thous* and the *haths*. The mannered Biblical language was not "holy" as such. It was "contemporary" in its time too.

Do not be ashamed to pray. It is a sign of strength, not weakness. Chances are you have prayed many times, often in desperation, when some sudden threat or adversity confronted you. *Don't wait until your life is on the line. Don't pray as a last resort. Pray as a first cause.* Pray to set a new direction in your life. Prayers are profoundly believed thoughts. They are the architect's plans for the better life you wish to build.

Once you have affirmed your prayer with belief, release your businesslike subconscious mind to do its work. Don't try to tell it how to do its job. Your subconscious mind is an infinite storehouse of practical ideas. It works with absolute logic—if you do not impede it.

I spoke to a friend recently who had been very successful. Like many, the recession had seriously affected his business. His accounts payable had risen alarmingly. His accounts receivable had fallen dangerously. Unpaid bills were piling up. The bank he had dealt with for years reassessed the liquidity of his business and found that its assets no longer met the minimum loan requirements.

"I tried to use your Imaginology gimmick, or whatever you call it," he said, "and so far nothing has happened."

When he added "gimmick" I knew what the problem was. Like so many others when we are faced with a crisis and have the greatest need for help, we negate the result with sneaky little doubts.

You must let your request—your prayer—take root. Don't plant a request for help or guidance in your subconscious mind and then, ten minutes later, dig it up to see if it's growing!

Give it a chance. Some prayers are answered immediately. Others may take longer. So don't place still another limitation on your subconscious by trying to tell it how long and in what manner your prayer should be answered.

A week or so later this friend called again. His manner was contrite. "I'm sorry I was a doubter," he said. "I really worked hard and dug out the doubt like you said—and do you know what happened . . . ?"

"Of course," I replied. "You received an answer."

"I sure did!" he responded enthusiastically. "I woke up the other morning and, for some reason, I remembered a call I got from a fellow a few months back. He had a new process for compressing all sorts of non-polluting combustible refuse into stove and fireplace fuel. He wanted me to act as his distributor in this area.

"I found his number and called, figuring that by now he had solved his problem. But he hadn't. We talked wholesale and retail prices and margins and I discovered that his product could sell at 20 percent less than split wood or those fancy compressed logs and still leave room for everybody.

"I've got orders from two supermarket chains now and it looks like this one new line can double my business by next spring!"

How many times have you been faced with a problem— often just a small one—and you've wracked your brain for an answer?

Finally, in desperation, you decide to "sleep on it."

Then, lo and behold, the next morning an idea came out of "nowhere" and with it a solution.

You were *sure* the answer was there. You had *faith*. You did not *doubt*. As a result you gave your subconscious mind a clear command to bring the solution into your consciousness.

It did.

If your prayer is clear and reasonable and it is powered by complete belief—faith—that you'll get a right answer, you will.

6

Imaginology
and
Auto-Suggestion

---

*The "automatic transmission"
in your mind makes shifting
from negative to positive thought
and action so simple a small child can do it.
So take your mind out of "park"
and get on the high road
to happy living!*

If you have any doubts about hypnotism, try to set them aside for a few minutes. There is some clear light to be shed on this remarkable tool for reaching your subconscious mind and programming it to materialize all the good things you desire.

To begin with, prayer sincerely and frequently repeated is a form of positive self- or auto-hypnosis.

Since hypnotism is a very direct and effective way of reaching the subconscious mind, and since the subconscious mind does not make judgments, hypnotism can, of course, be used negatively also—with certain built-in moral limitations.

In a sense, the constant repetition of those scare ads we discussed earlier is a form of hypnosis—often a pernicious form. They are designed to condition us to believe that we are constantly threatened by all manner of disturbing things—illness, disease, death, accidents, poverty, and so on.

There are many forms and degrees of hypnosis. Anybody who has undertaken a long cross-country drive knows something of highway hypnosis, the dangerous state of semiawareness that can be induced by sitting in one position too long, by driving at the same speed too long, by not changing lanes to break the monotony, by allowing the center divider line to dominate your peripheral vision, or by continually listening to the monotonous beat of some of our contemporary music.

Highway patrolmen and troopers in every state of the union are agreed that many of the worst accidents they are forced to cover are caused by highway hypnosis and fatigue. They work hand in hand to create tragedy.

In an effort to divert a driver's attention and force him or her into a fresh state of awareness, some counties have varied the size, color, and shape of lane-dividing lines.

In some states, on particularly monotonous stretches of highway, drivers are required to keep their lights on during the day. A lot of lives have been saved.

Have you ever watched the fixed stares and the enraptured expressions on the faces of our young people at a rock concert? I still harbor some doubt as to whether or not they understand all of the lyrics. Even so, intelligible or not, the words become a part of the monotonous beat that, in itself, is a form of hypnosis.

Some critics who have analyzed the lyrics claim that they are actually subliminal messages related to narcotics and sex inserted into the mass subconscious of the listeners by way of the primitive rock-and-roll beat.

If so, it is an example of the negative use of Imaginology through repetitive conditioning of the subconscious.

Not long ago there were a number of feature articles in magazines claiming that even our printed advertising was subtly conditioning us to respond to a powerful basic urge—the urge to procreate—by injecting subliminal sex images in the illustrations of certain products. Two mentioned most frequently were cosmetics and alcoholic drinks.

Whether or not the charges were founded in fact, I do not know. But I spent ten years on advertising's "Mad" Avenue in New York. I learned something of the "diabolically clever" creative thinking of which my confreres were capable. At no time in the two agencies in which I served as a radio director-producer or as director of television was I ever asked to inject some "Sneaky Petes" into our commercials.

On the other hand, again recognizing the ingenuity of the creative minds in the business, it seems entirely possible that some genius suggested that such a rumor be started, totally without foundation, in order to increase readership of the ads by initiating some innocent voyeurism on the part of the readers! I wonder if the frustration engendered might not be self-defeating?

An example of hypnosis as a positive force is one that most

parents know well. At bedtime how many lovable little wheedlers have said, "Read me a story, Daddy"?

If Mommy or Daddy understand the principle of hypnosis, their soft, monotonous voices will soon set little heads to nodding. Bedtime stories are aptly named!

We hope you will agree that there is such a thing as the valid use of hypnosis and that it is not necessarily a bad or dangerous technique, as some claim—a device best suited to showmen who delight audiences with their "mystical powers."

Now, how can hypnosis in its several forms work for you? To begin with, there are literally thousands upon thousands of cases where hypnotherapy administered by a psychologist trained in the techniques has broken confirmed smokers of the habit. The same is true of drink. The same is true of inferiority complexes. The same is true of guilt complexes involving alleged infractions of so-called "moral laws"—sexual aberrations, either actually practiced or simply experienced as a frightening urge.

The psychologist, having lulled the patient into a state of deep relaxation, then uses a monotonous voice that is almost a chant of carefully chosen words that will produce the correct result in the patient's subconscious by replacing the negative concepts with positive ones.

The wonderful part about the process is this: You can do the same thing yourself in a great many instances by simply using the I.B.M. method.

We are not suggesting that you try self-hypnosis if you suspect you are suffering from a severe neurosis that seems beyond your ability to manage. In that case you must seek the help of an ethical, well-trained psychologist who knows how to steer you through the emotional morass of accumulated wrong thinking.

In most instances you can use auto- or self-hypnosis to reinforce those positive mental pictures that you wish to impress on your subconscious by way of enriching your life.

As an added help, when you first awaken, or better still, when you are about to go to sleep, you can repeat quietly to yourself just one word. Do it over and over again, not by rote. You must visualize what it stands for in materialized terms and feel the pleasure derived from its manifestation.

If you do not do that, you may be like the small child who is lulled to sleep by little more than the repetitive sound of a parent's voice.

If it is more money that you desire, repeat over and over the single word, "Wealth." Feel it flowing to you. Feel the pleasure of receiving it, the pleasure of using it to get those good things you need to make your life richer and easier.

If it is good health you yearn for, repeat the word "Health." Feel it being made manifest in your life. Aid the process for your subconscious by remembering and feeling again those joyous days when you were in good health.

If it is love you desire to give or receive,' repeat the word, "Love," over and over again and feel the wonderful warmth and excitement of loving and being loved in return.

If it is a better position you desire, repeat over and over again the words, "Perfect job."

The technique of constant repetition worked wonders for a famous popular singing star I worked with some years ago. She brought to this life an extraordinary native talent. Her voice and musicianship were inborn. Aside from some coaching, she needed very little help to go to the top of the charts.

But, she was not pretty in the Hollywood sense of the word. She was not a glamorous female, but she was far from unattractive. When she sang one could hear "the echo of angels" in her voice. More than that, she was a wonderful human being.

At a time when her contemporary female singers were either announcing their romances or getting married, my friend found herself spending too much time alone or in business meetings with arrangers and conductors or song pluggers. Essentially a homebody, she wanted more than anything else to have a husband and a home she could retreat to after strenuous weeks on the road.

When that wish seemed to be denied her she began to overeat. In a year's time she was nearly fifty pounds overweight. It began to tell in her club bookings. While her recording dates went on as usual, the very lucrative personal appearances in the big clubs dropped off. Finally, her manager could ignore the problem no longer and he told her the truth.

Frightened, she went to a number of health clubs and tried a number of reducing aids and diets. Nothing seemed to work until she went to a hypnotherapist, almost as a last resort.

Under hypnosis the therapist was able to get her to confess her fears about being unattractive and neglected. After a half dozen in-depth sessions in which he gave her post-hypnotic suggestions designed to make her feel positive about her appearance, he did something that was pure Imaginology at work. He told her to sit in a comfortable place, surround herself with the best of the many professional photos she used in her business when she was slim, then concentrate on seeing herself that way again.

"When you look in the mirror from now on," he said, "don't see the heavy image reflected there. Instead, imagine yourself as you want to look again. Do it several times each day. And tell yourself that you are attractive and that you have an exceptional talent and that people are drawn to you. Tell yourself that, and *believe it! Believe it! It's true!*"

Skeptical at first, my young singer friend gave it a half-hearted try. When she went back to the therapist some weeks later he charged her with disbelief and said, "If I wanted to I could keep on taking your money for months, but that's not the sort of reputation I want. Now go back again, get out the photos and see yourself slim and lovely, for that's what you once were."

He glanced at the autographed picture of her on the wall by his desk. "And let me tell you something, Miss _____, if I were not old enough to be your grandfather, I'd be backstage every night with a bouquet myself. Not only are you one hell of a talent, young lady, but you are also one of the most attractive patients I've had, and you know who recommended me so you know I know some very pretty ladies!"

The talk did the trick. She went back to the routine again, and this time she stuck to it. At first the pounds melted slowly but as dresses got looser and had to be refitted and as old gowns began to fit again and show off a really lovely figure, she found her belief reinforced.

In four months she had shed thirty pounds. In six months she was back to her old measurements again. A year later, while singing in one of the big casinos, she met a young orchestra leader who finally confessed that he'd been admiring her from afar for several years.

They started to date, fell in love, and got married. Until she retired, they worked together, "collaborated" on two children, and today are one of the most respected couples in the business. The lady, now in her "fairest forties," will begin recording again soon and I have no doubt that still more Gold Records are destined for her study wall.

But be sensible in your requests. If you are starting in the steno pool or the mail room, don't expect your subconscious to come up with an instant promotion to executive secretary or vice president. While those promotions are entirely possible they usually come as the result of sustained good service to the company. Aspire, of course, but be willing to take your promotions one at a time—to earn them.

In the case of health and love, "instant" answers are quite often possible. The so-called "miracle healings" are an example of absolute faith. "Love at first sight" is not a romantic dream. It can and does happen, usually as the result of the lovers' faith that it will. The reincarnationists will tell you that it happens when you meet an old love from a past life. I would not dispute that. But even if so, the subconscious belief that the meeting will take place is undoubtedly the reason it does.

So, to reinforce the process of using Imaginology to enrich your life, you should take the key word from your longer request—your prayer—and repeat it over and over again, using the self-hypnotic technique to further inculcate your subconscious mind.

It is worth saying again that no hypnotist, not even a charlatan, can force you to do something that is against your principles while in a hypnotic state.

You might, with your consent, be made to bark like a dog, do a tap dance, crow like a rooster, or even become a human bridge between two chairs while someone stands on your middle without collapsing you. But you cannot be persuaded or forced to do anything that you feel is wrong. You must consciously consent to be put into a hypnotic state.

If you fear hypnosis—a most useful tool when ethically used—remember that!

Once again, because health and love are the dominant preoccupations with most of us, hypnosis can be, and is, a most effective tool.

Persons suffering from obesity have had their reasons for a negative self-image uncovered under hypnosis and have been relieved and returned to their old happy lifestyle, freed of their hangups.

Persons suffering from sexual hangups and disfunctions have been cured almost miraculously by therapists who understood that most often these painful and embarrassing problems are mental and not physical.

There is another aspect having to do with age. The problem of satisfactory sex is particularly painful for older persons who have been programmed since their early years to believe that as rheumatism and wrinkles appear the romantic twinkle disappears. *Not so!*

Just as overprotective parents often used to warn their offspring that "sex is all in your head," so have we been warned that lack of sexual desire is to be expected after fifty. That is a cruel and negative allegation that has no foundation in a normal, healthy older body. The plus-minus factor in the old equation "use it or lose it" is far closer to the truth.

Sex with a loving, willing and respected partner can be most effective physical and emotional therapy. Nothing tempts Father Time to hang up his hourglass more than the continued youthful, enthusiastic attitude toward love and loving.

Recently an eighty-year-old widower I know, after some live-in years with his seventy-three-year-old widowed lady friend, decided to get married.

"What the heck," he said, "obviously I'm not going to die young so to hell with the social security savings. We might as well make it legal."

As they left the church the radiant bride was heard to say, "Do you have the tickets, Harry?" When he patted his pocket and reassured her she squeezed his arm and whispered, "Okay, love, let's get to New York and get it on!"

The truth is, apart from highway hypnosis and negative news and scare ads, we are victimizing ourselves a good part of the time with self-hypnosis.

We do it each time we persist in thinking negative thoughts. Each time we embrace such thoughts we are engaged in a subtle form of self-hypnosis that sends negative signals to our subconscious minds.

That means we have to monitor our thought patterns if we are not to negate those positive impressions that we send to our subconscious minds during our conscious use of the principle of Imaginology.

Remember this: *We are not at the mercy of negative outside influences unless we believe ourselves to be.* We are subject to the blessings of our "inside influences" when we dismiss the harmful impressions around us by denying them credibility and when, as Johnny Mercer and Harold Arlen wrote in their great popular hit, we "Accent-tchu-ATE the Positive."

It was back in 1944 when that hit was introduced in the film, *Here Come the Waves.* As a nation we *did* accentuate the positive—and we won that war.

In our personal conflicts we may lose a battle now and then, but if we are consistent in the use of the principles of Imaginology, we'll win the war.

7

Imaginology
and Success

*If at first you don't succeed,
change your thinking. That's all
you need!*

Most of us have a fairly clear idea of the meaning of the word success. Out of curiosity I decided to consult a dependable and indispensable friend of mine, *Websters New International Dictionary.*

There's an inch of fine print in the definition, the net of which is this:

> *Degree or measure of succeeding, or attaining one's desired end—a succeeding fully or in accordance with one's desires.*

The first part implies the possibility of a limited success. The second part says quite clearly, "a succeeding fully . . ." which seems to contradict the first part—until you read on—"in accordance with one's desires."

In short, success can be relative. You can achieve an objective to the full measure of your hopes and dreams and say, in all truth, "I am a success."

You have achieved "in accordance with your desires." You have materialized all the things you imagined in your mental picture. You programmed your subconscious to the extent that it materialized all that you asked for. You *are*, in fact, successful.

We have a very successful family bakery nearby. In the morning there is usually a line at the door. Men and women on their way to work are eager to have coffee and a freshly baked Danish or a delicious flaky strudel or croissant.

Some time ago an official of a large baking company offered to buy out the family and all of its recipes.

The father, a master baker trained in Europe, thanked the man and said, "Why should we? We are a success here. We do not want to be as big as National Biscuit" (not the company that made the offer, by the way). *His success was a complete and satisfying reality to him.*

My brother, a retired "country banker" living in northern Washington State, is a hunter. He hunts only for the table. Not once has he failed to bring back his big game bag.

Not so with the others. When they ask how he does it, he replies, "I close my eyes, see that big buck or moose, then I go where he is."

When his less fortunate friends come to his door for a gift of steaks and ribs and roasts from his freezer, my brother explains his success in another way.

"I guess," he says, "that you're beating a path to my door because I built a better 'moose trap.'"

Actually, they were there because when they had come back empty-handed they had programmed themselves for possible defeat.

"Moose are getting scarce . . .". "Been out three winters now. Didn't see nuthin' but cows." "Too many hunters—too little game."

My brother "just knew"—never doubted—that he'd get his game. He not only visualized his quarry but he saw it efficiently butchered to provide many nourishing meals for family and friends, and he anticipated the pleasure of sharing.

In his remote, wild, and beautiful Mt. Baker wilderness country, wild game, especially deer, are plentiful—a welcome substitute for expensive, hard-to-come-by beef.

The one thing above all that blocks success is the fear of failure.

Now, if the following appears to be a digression, you will see in a moment that it is not.

The fear of failure often has its roots in a sense of rejection since the one thing we need above all is to be valued and loved.

In this sad time of thousands upon thousands of single-parent families, the children who are the innocent victims of those broken homes are going to need special consideration as they grow into adulthood.

With one parent, usually the father, opting out of the marriage—and the reasons are myriad if not always valid—these youngsters must feel a sense of desertion, a sense of rejection.

Unless they have very perceptive parents and relatives who anticipate their emotional need for attention and take steps to prevent the problems that result, we could have a hoard of rejected young people trying as best they can to survive, to achieve a sense of self worth and to make a place for themselves.

The feeling of rejection partially explains the so-called Beat Generation of the Forties and the Hippie movement of the Fifties and early Sixties.

Their costumes and their customs are really a bid for the attention they lacked in their early years.

After talking to them and writing a novel, with their sincere help, in which their lifestyle was explored, I am certain they grouped together in an effort to create for themselves the sense of family they were denied.* (Punk rock is another example.)

Narcotic "highs" helped them forget, temporarily, their emotional wounds. The "square" society had rejected them. Their answer was a counterculture in which they made the rules.

Regardless of the generation you belong to, every war and every depression or recession has taken its toll on families. Emotional and economic problems reinforce each other. The result is uncertainty and fear.

So it is not a digression to dig a little to discover why fear can have such deep roots.

So many who seek out and read "How to Succeed" books do so because they suspect they are not, or cannot be, successful. To suspect something is to fear it. *The only way to root out that fear is to reprogram the subconscious mind.*

Your subconscious mind does not love you or hate you or feel sorry for you. *It does not judge.* It is completely neutral in that sense. But there is one thing you may be certain of—*it will never desert you!* In that truth lies the unending comfort—the ultimate security—and the only way out of your dilemma.

The opportunities to meet a need and succeed in this world are endless. To find the opportunity that best suits you requires a

*Leland Frederick Cooley. *The Art Colony*. New York: Avon, 1975.

little elementary logic. If you are afraid of high places, don't decide to be a steeple jack! If you are afraid of the water don't try to be a sailor. Don't try to be any of those things that you deeply fear.

Think carefully and clearly about those vocations that most appeal to you, the ones you could give yourself to with interest and enthusiasm, the ones for which you think you have a "special feel." More about that in a moment. But let's go back to fear.

Some people, perhaps a great many, have a need to face fear and conquer it to bolster their self-esteem. Good! Anything you do that increases your worth in your own eyes will also increase your worth in the eyes of others.

Why? Because you "licked a problem" and grew taller on the inside! Taller in your own estimation. As a result you commanded the attention and respect and admiration of others.

You might even discover that you like being a steeple jack, or working "high iron" after you conquered your fear of high places!

So, if you have some things that you feel you need to prove to yourself, and they are not foolish things that may jeopardize your safety and the happiness of your loved ones, then "go for it!" The name of the game of life is growing.

The "bottom line" is this: *The logical thing, the sensible thing to tackle is that which will offer you the greatest favorable odds for success.* That's why it is important to examine your heart and choose realistically one of the things you feel most comfortable with.

In considering odds, it is far more than a trifling truism to remember that any task that fills the basic needs of a great many people—supplies a critical service—is likely to be one that offers the greatest potential opportunity.

Of course, others may be working to fill such a need or provide such a service. But if you are determined to know more about your clients' (customers') needs and do more to fill them, you will find you've built that legendary "better mousetrap."

How do you go about deciding which of your choices is the one to concentrate on? Use the basic communication with your subconscious. Recognize its presence in you. Acknowledge with all your faith its ability to provide you with the right answers to honestly asked questions.

Another technique that you can safely and easily use to communicate with your subconscious involves the use of a simple device, the pendulum.

There are two or three most direct ways to communicate with your subconscious. The pendulum is one. Automatic writing is another, and the time honored Ouija board is still another.

Now, please, if you are tempted to think that these next few paragraphs smack of some sort of quackery or questionable "magic," try to keep an open mind. Try to remember that if we are to expand our knowledge, *the most fearsome sound in the world is the clanging shut of a closed mind.*

Closed minds kept our world as the center of the universe until Copernicus proved that we and the other planets in our solar system actually revolve around the sun.

Closed minds held that the earth was flat until Columbus and Magellan proved that it was round.

The use of ideamotor techniques to contact the subconscious mind is centuries old, far older than a lot of the pseudoscientific "fortunetelling" methods that pretend to predict your future. The pendulum device for directly contacting your subconscious is by far the easiest and one of the most dependable available to us at present.

Here is how it works and what it can do: Take a ring or a washer or a small weight of any sort and secure it to the end of an eight- or ten-inch length of light string or heavy thread.

Now hold it between your thumb and index finger so that it dangles over a flat surface and brace your elbow comfortably to make a steady foundation for the suspended pendulum.

As an example of how it will work when your subconscious mind begins to move it, consciously swing it gently in a small arc toward you and away from you. Then swing it in an arc from left to right. Now swing it in a small clockwise circle. Then swing it in a counterclockwise circle. It can also be swung diagonally right and left but those are not moves that commonly occur.

Having familiarized yourself with the feel of the little pendulum and the directions it may take, choose one of the directions to mean, "Yes" to your question. The opposite direction will mean "No." A third direction—one of the circles—will mean "I don't know" and the opposite circle will mean, "I don't care to answer."

You can choose whichever direction you wish to mean whatever you want it to mean, or—and many practitioners feel this is best—you can ask the pendulum (your subconscious) which direction it prefers for its answers.

Whatever your choice, you'll get answers and, remember, the responses will not be coming from your conscious mind. You will not move the pendulum. You will hold it as steady as humanly possible. The responses will come from undetectable involuntary muscle reactions initiated by your subconscious.

All right. You are ready to start now:

Hold the pendulum an inch or so above the surface of the table or desk. Do not consciously try to influence the direction of the motion to get the answer you most desire. If possible, hold your arm and hand rock steady. You can brace your wrist with your free hand as long as you do not restrict the motion of the pendulum.

It is not necessary to help your subconscious function. If you doubt this, remember that it is your subconscious mind that keeps all of the involuntary functions of your body in operation. You do not have to ask it to keep your heart beating. You do not have to ask it to keep your breathing going and to keep your lungs on the job extracting oxygen from the air and delivering it to your blood stream.

All of these involuntary functions in our remarkably complicated bodies are managed by our subconscious minds without our conscious help. Awake or asleep, they never leave the job.

Is it surprising then, that an intelligence that can manage so many things at once should have no trouble at all causing some involuntary motions in your pendulum?

With the pendulum in position you are now ready to ask your subconscious mind for some answers. Again, do not confuse it with multiple questions. Ask one at a time and try to limit your questions to two or three at the most.

If your principal interest is in changing your job and you want to know whether or not the one you envision is the best for you, say aloud (or think) "I am considering (describe the job briefly). It is one that appeals to me. Is it the best choice? Am I making a correct decision?"

You must have unquestioning faith that your subconscious knows everything about your strengths and your weaknesses, your true wishes and desires, and your talents and aptitudes.

You must know that it will process, in seconds, all of the pertinent data, assess the relative effectiveness of such personal data, and come up with the answer. *Moreover, you must believe that the answer will always be right.*

If you are wondering whether or not you should choose a partner—a husband or a wife or a business associate—ask your subconscious this through the pendulum: "Am I making the best possible choice in this person?" *Keep the questions simple, clear and direct.*

If you are wondering about the wisdom of an investment, ask your subconscious this: "I am considering (such and such a move). Is it the wisest choice I can make? Should I make it now?"

Remember this: The pendulum is not a *fortune telling device.* Do not ask it to predict the future. Do not ask it to pick winning teams in sports, or the winning horse in a race, or the winning fighter in a boxing match. If you want possible answers to such questions read the dope sheets pertaining to those sports and draw your own conclusions from the track records. It's far safer and surer and far less costly.

When your pendulum indicates that your subconscious is not certain, try rephrasing the question. If it is still not certain, drop the effort until you have done some more thinking about the problem.

If the pendulum indicates that it does not wish to answer, say, "If I do some more thinking, will you answer later?"

If the reply is negative, do not force it. It will probably be wiser to heed a flat turndown and let your aspirations seek another direction.

I have talked with a number of hypnotherapists and not one of them is willing to say that the subconscious can peer into the future. By inference, though, it does "predict" the future when it confirms your choice of a job or a partner or the rightness of some other request. If you follow that course, your "future" success is assured.

So, there's no mystical force involved in using the pendulum. Neither is there in automatic writing or the use of the Ouija board or the planchette.

If you are not familiar with the technique of automatic writing, you will find it is similar to the Ouija board, except that instead of a board one uses a large pad or a roll of paper. Instead of the little planchette that scoots around to spell out sentences the pencil held lightly in the writing hand moves across the paper to achieve the same function.

Here again, it is the subconscious that is responding to your questions. Here again, no predictions and no frivolous questions. You'll get nothing!

There is a variation of the pendulum that works on much the same principle. It is called finger lifting. In this case you sit in a relaxed position with your arms and hands resting comfortably on a table or on the arms of a chair.

You ask your subconscious questions precisely as you asked them for the pendulum. The answers will come when a finger lifts involuntarily.

Usually a right index finger lifting means "Yes." A left one means, "No." A thumb lifting means, "I do not know," and the little finger lifting means, "I do not care to answer."

For most people the pendulum is the easiest and most satisfactory method of contacting the subconscious quickly and directly.

Some people have trouble getting responses with any method. But hardly anyone fails if they are persistent and sincere in their wish to get an answer. The encouraging thing is this: By far the greatest majority of people who use the pendulum are successful within a very short time, usually in a matter of minutes.

This is important. If you feel self-conscious or uncomfortable, if you have any reservations about the validity of these methods, do not try them. The doubt will negate any possible good result.

On the other hand, if you can approach these methods of contacting your subconscious with an open mind—by saying to yourself, "I will not prejudge. I will not scoff. I am willing to give it an honest try"—you will most likely get enough evidence to make you an enthusiastic believer very quickly.

Remember this: Thousands of physicians, psychologists, psychiatrists, dentists, veterinarians (yes!), and therapists use the many forms of hypnosis and ideamotor techniques to solve problems that seem beyond the ability of their patients. Hypnosis is often used as an anesthetic in dentistry, minor operations, and childbirth.

Once you have come to accept and rely on one of the forms of self-hypnosis, you will never be without the good counsel of your mental "board of directors," your subconscious. If you wish to investigate further the subject of hypnosis as an ethical tool to help you make right decisions, there are a number of excellent books available.

In my public library I found six of them, all written by qualified practitioners. They make fascinating and reassuring reading.

As this was being written I received a call from a writer friend, a man who has had one internationally known best-selling novel. It had been made into a highly successful motion picture.

Since that first big success he has had only indifferent success with subsequent novels. His frustration has been mounting steadily.

At lunch several months ago he told me he had at least three ideas he was "excited" about but he was reluctant to commit time to them because, to quote him, "I'm always excited about any idea I feel like writing! The trouble is, lately my editors have said they did not feel the stories were right for today's market—whatever that means. I've got to write to live, but which one do I gamble on?"

I replied, "Why gamble? Why not let your subconscious editor make the choice for you?"

He looked at me as though I'd suddenly slipped my trolley. When I explained the use of the pendulum and how the infinite knowledge of the subconscious can help make the right decision, he shook his head uncertainly. "What have I got to lose?"

I rigged up a pendulum for him, and showed him how to use it by demonstrating it myself.

He watched my arm and hand closely for a time. "Well, I don't know if it'll work for me, but I know that you were not moving your arm or hand so there must be something to it."

I told him to boil down the theme of each of the three stories and ask the pendulum to respond to the questions, "Is story A the one I should develop for today's market?" "Is story B the one?" "Is story C the one?"

"Go home and practice for a while until you get over your self-consciousness," I advised. "Then give it an honest, unskeptical try."

He did.

The telephone call I just received was to say that Story B was the one the pendulum indicated. He had done a ten-page outline and sent it off to his literary agent who had forwarded it to New York.

"The editor called the day they received the outline," he said with obvious excitement. "They are really 'high' on the story and (he named his representative) is working out a good contract. If that pendulum works like that, I'm going to write nothing but best sellers!"

His reaction was predictable but I had to caution him that all the pendulum had done was relay to his conscious mind what his subconscious mind knew was the story he would do best.

Because that hapened to be true he had done a fine job of presenting the outline and the positive "vibes" had been transmitted to the editor, who had responded accordingly.

It is no guarantee of perpetual best sellers, but certainly a guarantee that he will have picked the story he can do best!

I've taken the time to tell this real-life story because it is a fine example of how your subconscious can help you make a decision where a *multiple choice* is involved.

If the decision is left only to conscious "reason," it can be influenced by a great many emotional factors, some of which may be concerned with what others will think of your decision—your image—your status among family and friends. In other words, which job presents you in the "best light," not which job is the one that will be most satisfying to you.

In the end the best job will be the one that you can do best and that is the one that will present you in the best light—to yourself!

The chances are far better than ever that your success will result in the admiration of all those who really count, and that is all that *really* counts.

8

Imaginology
and Money

*There's solid gold
in the treasury of your mind.
Unlock your mental vault
and get it.*

Except for health, there is hardly anything more frequently thought about or more controversial than money.

In First Timothy 6:10 we are told that "The love of money is the root of all evil."

On the other hand, George Bernard Shaw found "the lack of money . . ." to be "the root of all evil."

Money, in itself, is never evil. It is the symbol of services performed. It is the nature of the service that is either blessed or damned. To malign the rich is to betray your envy. There is no surer way to obstruct the flow of riches to yourself than to envy those who have made the subconscious mind serve their wishes for affluence by applying the principles of Imaginology to bring abundance into their lives.

Conversely, there is no surer way to remove that obstruction than to cast out your jealousy and envy and honestly rejoice in their good fortune.

You may ask, "What about the gangsters, and the dope dealers and swindlers, and all of the others who seem to make vast fortunes preying on the weaknesses of others?"

Pause for a moment and think about the lives they live. Could you really envy them? Endlessly hunted—never a moment of real peace? Inevitably, violent ends?

Remember, the subconscious mind knows neither good nor evil. It makes no judgment. It simply materializes what the conscious mind directs it to do and believes implicitly that it will be done.

How can that be? It is very simple. If your negative thoughts can program your subconscious to produce negative experiences in your life, and if the subconscious does not judge good or evil, why should it be surprising that it cares not at all whether what you believe in is "good" or "evil"? It does not make that distinction. Our society makes it.

I've asked many people to define evil. The simplest, clearest definition for me came from a lay preacher, a Moseslike man who ranched near my family in northern California. He said, "Evil is any thought or act that diminishes the dignity of the Holy Spirit in Man."

Again, would you really trade places with any of the crime leaders who must live in constant terror of the law or of their own kind who covet their territory, and will "finger" them, and let a contract out on them? There is no more uptight group of people in this world than the racketeers who control billions in illicit drug, gambling, and prostitution traffic. They live outside the protection of our law and in constant fear of the consequences of their own law that condones the wanton killing of any person who is a threat to their operations, inside the "family" or out.

Think a moment. No matter how great your need for money, could you really envy them their millions, perhaps billions?

The choice is yours. You can ask for the good things in life and say, "Let us pray," or you can opt for the evil that is the root of their riches and say, "Let us *prey.*"

Earlier, it was shown how to use Imaginology to find your place in life, if you feel that you are not in it at present.

Let's assume now that you are doing the thing you want to do as your life work, but you need to do it better and in so doing make more money to care for yourself and your loved ones.

How does Imaginology work to produce this result?

Go back again to the three steps made easy to remember by the three letters: I.B.M.

I for Imagine
B for Believe
M for Materialize

It makes no difference how you remember the steps. Neither does it make any difference if you call the creative process Imaginology, or Divine Manifestation, or Divine Demonstration, or simply Healing.

The only thing that counts is following the three steps. They are absolutely essential if you would materialize in your life those good things that you want.

Earlier, we used the example of visualizing the house of your dreams. You saw it. You felt it. You believed that it exists now. You asked your subconscious mind to materialize it. The same exact process works in visualizing abundance in your life.

You have heard the old saying, "He's stumbling over dollars to pick up dimes." Those unseen dollars that we stumble over are just as real as the dimes we stoop to pick up. More than that, it does not take ten times the effort to go for the dollars. All it takes is a little enlarging of the mental picture, a positive enlargement from the "ten-cent negative," and *belief.*

If your money comes from a fixed paycheck, a salary that has been determined by management's concept of the importance of your position, or if your paycheck comes from a wage scale fixed by your union, it may seem like an exercise in futility to ask your subconscious to give you a raise.

When you are visualizing more money and security in your life it makes no difference what its source, so long as it is a legitimate and constructive one.

You can influence your corporate paycheck in time by determining to make yourself more valuable to the company. Imaginology works there very well indeed. Your image of a more important role will bring its reward if you power the image with belief.

You can influence your factory paycheck by determining to do your job better than the next person. Some of you will dispute that and say, "How can I be better than the machine I run? Twenty other guys and gals are running identical machines—turning out identical products or parts!"

That may very well be true. I myself was once a part of an assembly line in a tire factory. I know about those doubts!

It is difficult to stand out when you feel like a picket in a fence—when you feel your identity is lost, that you are just another time card. But there's always a way out, a way *up.*

I found a way that is still open and always will be to anybody who will use the principle of Imaginology to bring more pleasure and abundance into the life experience.

At age nineteen, after serving an apprenticeship on a tramp steamer in the South Pacific, Australia, New Zealand, and the

East Indies, I gave up the thought of emulating my Danish grand-father and becoming a ship's master.

I sailed in pre-union times. I gave up the dream because as an able-bodied seaman earning only $62.50 a month, I could not save up enough money to go to the Merchant Marine Academy to get a third mate's ticket, which is where a young officer starts.

The country was in the depths of the Great Depression. College graduates were selling apples on street corners and living in packing cases and tarpaper shacks unjustly called, "Hoovervilles."

Ruined speculators who fueled the boom market with their greed were diving out of office windows on Wall Street and the lines were at the missions and soup kitchens, not at the movie houses.

After a discouraging period I landed a job in a tire factory in Southern California at twenty-five cents an hour, ten hours a day, six days a week. It seemed like a fortune!

After a few months on the tube assembly line (they had inner tubes and flaps and demountable rims in those days) I was transferred to the second floor to run a gum dipping machine.

This involved taking steel reels of bead, the reinforced edge of the casing that goes against the rim, and dipping the strips in a solution of rubber dissolved in a highly volatile solvent. It was so strong it burned my eyes and lungs and literally took the skin from my hands.

After a week I had two choices—either quit and join thousands of others on the job lines, or find a better way to do it.

One thing you do on a tramp steamer is learn to improvise. Suddenly an idea came. Instead of scraping the excess liquid rubber from the beads by hand, I went to the machine shop and talked an old world craftsman—a pattern maker who cut tread impressions in steel molds—to make me some dies that I could thread the bead through to strip off the excess gum.

I took the gadget upstairs and rigged it over the tank.

It worked like a charm.

A week went by. Suddenly the superintendent showed up. He was wearing a puzzled expression. I had about twenty reels of bead stacked on the hand truck ready to go down to the tire building line.

He looked around for a moment and then said, "How many men are working on this machine?"

"Just me, sir," I replied.

"Well, what in hell are you doing, working three shifts? They're up to their backsides in beads down on the line and the gum's drying out so it won't bond with the casings."

I showed him my raw hands and pointed to the dies. He studied the gadget for a few minutes then turned to me with a bemused smile.

"They can't keep up with you downstairs. You've got to slow down. Go down there and get those reels and run them through again. Then knock off and come to my office."

My heart sank. I had visions of the fo'cas'le again—the rotten food—the deadly monotony of chipping and painting and soojeing, the frustration of going ashore in glamorous ports with only pennies in my pocket—I would have bet he was going to chew me out and give me my walking papers.

Instead I found the superintendent, Mr. Pittinger, and the plant manager waiting for me.

I got a commendation for my "invention" and a new job as an assistant timekeeper at almost twice the pay—forty-seven cents an hour!

I also got a good lesson: Let the boss in on your plans, and, no matter how menial or unpleasant the job, look for a better way to do it—for yourself and for the company.

Your subconscious mind will be your best help there too. Ask it to show you the opportunities and it will. *But you must believe.*

Most factories have Management-Labor Quality Committees now, groups formed to upgrade both product and procedures—a very good place to have your constructive ideas recognized.

The additional money you need does not necessarily have to come from your job in the form of larger paychecks. It can come from many sources. Your subconscious knows all of them. It knows the ones that are right to fill your special needs. Generally speaking, it is better not to visualize the money coming from a specific source. That is not to say that it's impossible for that to happen, especially if you have a clear picture of the source and hold a firm conviction that it is a good and reasonable source of added income.

By far the best way is not to outline. Again—do not tell your subconscious how to do its job. Don't tell it when and where to make its deliveries! Instead, get yourself quiet and relaxed and say something like this:

> I have a need for more money in order to provide well for my family and insure a full and happy life for us all. Money is the recognition for work well done. I shall do all I can to deserve it. I am grateful for the opportunity to earn it. I shall use it well and unselfishly. I ask now for help in bringing the right opportunity into my life. I believe without question that the right opportunity will be shown to me.

It is not necessary to use those exact words. In fact, sometimes when we learn words "by heart" they are not "by heart" at all. They become automatic—familiar sounds mechanically repeated.

Make up your own request to your subconscious. Vary it but keep the sense the same, and keep it simple and clear.

What you are asking is an opportunuity to increase your income either through a raise for work well done on the job or through some supplementary source that does not conflict with your other responsibilities.

By the way, the subconscious mind "admires" responsibility in that you feel better about yourself when you know you are acting responsbily. You are more self-assured, more certain that you can accomplish your objectives. That belief lends impetus and power to the subconscious and expedites its assistance.

You can vary the words while still keeping the sense of them. Think about what they mean. Motivate them with conviction, with profound belief that they are being "heard" by your subconscious and will be acted upon.

This prayer for plenty *will* be acted upon, often in most unexpected and exciting ways.

I have a friend who is an expert gemologist. He was trained as an engineer. Gems and mineral specimens were his hobby but he dreamed that one day they would become his principal vocation. In fact, he knew it would.

In time it did. Naturally!

His reputation grew and so did his dream. He opened a modest shop. Many famous collectors began coming there and his reputation grew. So did his shop.

And then one day a stranger, a man in his middle years dressed much like a prospector, came into his shop carrying an old burlap bag. It was obviously concealing something quite heavy.

He asked to show it to my friend but insisted it be revealed in his private office away from prying eyes. Curious, my friend ag eed.

Several minutes later he burst out of the office, wide-eyed. The stranger was still seated inside.

"You won't believe this," he said, "but I've got to raise a lot of money immediately!"

When the sum was beyond my friend's ability at the moment he said, "It's a long shot, but I've got to try the bank."

While the mysterious stranger with his more mysterious burlap bundle cooled his heels in the inner office, my friend ran across the street to the bank.

In less than thirty minutes he was back, smiling with obvious relief.

"I told them what it was and they gave me a loan," he said as he disappeared into the office again.

To end the suspense, what he had bought was one of the world's largest gold nuggets.

It weighed well over thirteen pounds!

At the present market price this beautiful nugget is worth over a hundred thousand dollars.

As a prime specimen it is probably worth a quarter of a million dollars or more.

During the past several years it has been on exhibition at a dozen great museums, including the Smithsonian Institution in Washington, D.C.

With a dedicated punster's usual token apology, my friend calls the nugget his "Golden Opportunity."

By using the simple principles of Imaginology you can experience your own golden opportunities too. Like my friend, it may come unexpectedly through an opportunity to make a sound investment. It may be a modest one in the beginning with a potential for a large increase.

It may come as an idea with commercial value, something that fits an existing need. Or it may come with an inheritance, or a gift, or a settlement of some just claim.

The principal thing to remember is the importance of visualizing what you need. Of course you can visualize the actual money—checks, coins, drafts—but it is best to visualize the condition you wish to create that can best be materialized by a *sufficient source of money*.

In other words, imagine clearly and in detail what you want to accomplish with the money. Hold that image in your mind when you ask your subconscious to provide for your needs.

No matter what you wish to materialize with the help of your subconscious it always comes back to the application of the I.B.M. principle. Imagine and believe.

Do not ask your subconscious if it will do something for you. Don't ask it to "do you a favor."

Tell it, but don't order it like a Marine Corps D.I. paralyzing a platoon of new "skinheads." But don't be timid either and couch your request—your prayer—in uncertain language. Don't ask for your request to be deferred to some time in the future. Don't say, "If you're too busy now you can do it later . . ." The subconscious does not put orders "on the hook" to be filled at some future date. It begins to act the moment it receives the request. The clearer the vision the sooner the result.

If somebody is trying to explain something to you and that person hems and haws, and searches for words, and sounds uncertain, you may grow impatient or at least never get a clear idea of the thing.

The same reaction takes place in the subconscious, if you are indefinite about your request.

Imagine or envision clearly. Believe in the working of the principle—believe devoutly—without a shred of doubt.

Because you are human, if there be doubt, *root it out!*

9

Imaginology, Health, and Habits

We are not "stuck"
with lack of anything good except as
we believe we are.

The subconscious mind, by its very nature, is dedicated to keeping your body in perfect working order.

Its whole thrust is in that direction.

It will accomplish its purpose, unless you reprogram your subconscious to reflect illness or incapacity of any sort.

Because we are continually assailed in the media by visions of a score of dreadful ailments and misfortunes that can only be avoided if we buy this or that or do this or that, it is very easy for us to become victims of subliminal brainwashing campaigns. Do we have to look any further than political campaigns to judge their effectiveness? By the way, campaign is also the word used to describe an aggressive war! So it does not seem unreasonable to suggest that these advertising campaigns are really aggressive wars aimed at defeating the divine optimism of our subconscious minds where our health is concerned.

This is not to suggest that all ad campaigns are designed to inspire fear in us. There are many very successful ones that hope to better our own self-images. However, few of these seem to involve food and medicine.

So, we must be consciously on guard against visiting those negative thoughts on our subconscious minds—that singular subconscious mind that we all share. We must be alert for our own well-being and for the well-being of those we love, for it is entirely possible to transmit those fears to others as well.

How can that be?

The same principle applies when we visualize a family member or a dear friend as being ill or in danger. Just as we can be healed by thought—our own or those of a healer that we believe in implicitly—so can we become healers-in-reverse by holding over others those negative thought patterns.

71

Have you ever wondered about those instantaneous healings, those "miracles" that hapen so frequently at the famous shrines around the world?

Skeptics say, "Bunk! Superstition! Foolishness! It's all in their minds!"

Strangely enough, although the doubters' observations were totally negative, they were right when they said, "It's all in their minds."

The healings did and do take place because the supplicants went, often at great personal pain and expense, believing they would be healed. Those of unquestioning faith were healed.

This sort of "pure faith" often brings about similar miracles at revival meetings. The late Katherine Kuhlman effected many authenticated healings in her revival meetings around the country. The controversial evangelist, Aimee Semple McPherson, despite her personal notoriety, effected many such healings. These happen because both the patient and the healer do not doubt for an instant that a healing can be effected.

Here again, as it does all through the practice of Imaginology, the three-part principle we abbreviate as I.B.M. operates.

Imagine—believe—materialize. The operative word is always the same—*Belief*.

It is worth a few lines to discuss superstition—black cats, Friday the Thirteenth, walking under ladders, stepping on sidewalk lines, and the like. There are hundreds of them! They all serve to illustrate the negative side of the principle of Imaginology.

In Pennsylvania and New Jersey superstition is such a reality in the lives of some good country people that they often wear amulets and decorate their houses and barns with mystical symbols thought to ward off a hex.

There are some very interesting books and articles written on superstition. In them one finds some amusing stories, but the tragic consequences of superstition usually predominate.

Why is such "foolishness" given so much credibility? Because, for those who really believe in superstitions, all of the dire predictions *can happen* unless steps are taken to exorcise the demons.

Again, the subconscious does not care one whit how foolish or illogical your belief may be. If you really believe it, that's what you get dished up in your life.

Good or bad—the choice is always yours!

One of the commonest and most pernicious negatives is the myth of mandatory heredity. This does not mean size, coloring, or other obvious genetic printouts. Strangely enough, if we come from a line of long-lived people who were super intellects, outstanding achievers who distinguished themselves in their professions, we are only too happy to identify with them.

"Thank God I come from a long line of smart people," we hear them say. The very belief—and it is probably true—is enough to convince them of their mental superiority.

Such persons may drop their eyelashes with dull thuds of becoming modesty but, the truth is, they believe and rejoice in their exceptional intellects or talents. As a result they have developed them. I plus B plus M at work again. *Q.E.D.*

A reverse belief about the worth of our forebears can produce a negative result, unless you understand that you are not limited by the cerebral voltage of your kin folks. Superstition finds its way into this sort of thinking too. There is a common misconception that the size of the cranium determines the size of the intellect.

As a child I lived next door to a man with a great intellectual "dome." If there was any truth to the superstition that such a head must always accommodate an exceptional brain, the man would have been a Who's Who headliner. On the contrary, during the years I knew him there was little evidence that his noble dome was inhabited by any other than the most trivial thoughts.

In the next block was a kid we called "Pinhead." In the entire school of nearly two thousand students this slightly built lad with a head that seemed too small even for his undersized body stood at the head of the Dean's List during all four years. He later became a distinguished newspaper publisher and a behind-the-scenes political power.

If there is a moral it must be, "It's not the size of the container that counts. It's what you put in it."

Short of some birth defect, those tragic "accidents" that make us all bless our good bodies, there is no limit to the information, the knowledge, we can store in our heads, except, of course, the limitations we place on ourselves.

Your subconscious is not snobbish. It does not prefer to consort exclusively with superintellects. It is totally democratic. It will deal even-handedly if you identify with a genius or a defective forebear. "As a man thinketh," so will the subconscious make certain he is! Soaring intellect, plodding pedagoguery, or stultifying stupidity, it's all the same to the subconscious mind.

So it is that many people look back at their ailing forebears in an effort to assess their own longevity. We are aided in this negative exercise by medical and insurance questionnaires that have a morbid, actuarial interest in finding out what our parents and their parents and their brothers and sisters and aunts and uncles and cousins died from, and when.

Quite likely what happened in those past generations was a perversion of the principle of Imaginology. We are expected to inherit their weaknesses, physical and mental, and it is hoped that we will have inherited some of their good qualities too.

Euripides wrote, "The Gods visit the sins of the fathers upon the children." The Greek playwright may have cribbed the idea from Moses, who interpreted Jehovah as saying, ". . . for I, the Lord thy God, am a jealous God, visiting the iniquity of the fathers upon the children unto the third and fourth generation of them that hate me." Hate is interpreted to mean disbelieve.

There are a number of interpretations possible, but it does not seem unreasonable to imagine that God, speaking through His ancient prophet, meant that the ongoing "iniquity" was the guilty identification of the children with a father who never let them forget that his "sin" was to be shared by them. Such identification, if accepted as the unalterable truth, must cause the iniquity to be revisited down through the generations. The subconscious mind sees to that! Again, we are what we truly think we are, what we truly envision ourselves to be.

How do we use Imaginology to counter the negative images of ourselves where health is concerned? We do it by accepting the fact, without reservation, that the thrust of our subconscious mind, the entire drive of the miracle-working master mechanic that keeps our bodies going day and night without any overseeing from ourselves, is toward perfect health.

Every great teacher has found a way to say, "Thoughts are things."

By that they mean that you materialize, make into things, your deeply held thoughts.

It isn't necessary to vocalize your thoughts. Silent thoughts are just as potent as the most fervently uttered word.

One of the things that impresses a student of Imaginology is how varied are the healings that result from seeing and believing in the basic strength and good health of the human body.

Healings do not just alleviate or cure runny noses, hangnails, and drandruff. In fact, most healings have helped or brought about a remission of such major afflictions as cancer, tuberculosis, asthma, arthritis, chronic heart trouble, rheumatism, stomach and intestinal disorders, and a host of other serious illnesses.

This is not a generality but a matter of confirmed evidence. Healings have been effected, often after the sufferers have been told that medicine could do no more for them.

Without attempting to assess the medical worth of any of those potions or pills or injections, the miracle cures that receive such widespread press probably came about less from the efficacy of the medication than from the faith of the patient. This is not to suggest that they are, without exception, ineffective from a purely medical point of view. Laetril clinics are booming in Mexico. It *is* to say, however, that those patients who believed without reservation were healed. Others with lesser faith were helped a little and those who doubted but went as a last resort apparently got no help at all.

The most useful thing to remember when you are using Imaginology's principles to solve a problem or effect a healing is this: *Anything you can imagine actually exists in the realm of the mind.*

That is not an extravagant statement. Five hundred years ago Leonardo da Vinci conceived the first submarine, the first helicopter, the first hang glider, the first machine gun, the first hydraulic pump. And what about Jules Verne and *Twenty Thousand Leagues Under the Sea,* and those remarkable science fiction writers who "dreamed up" space probes, and shuttles, and intergalactic communications, and black holes, and all the rest?

It's all confirmed now!

When we are talking about materializing things in your life, we are not referring to what our young people refer to as "far out" things. We are talking about practical personal applications of the principle in our daily lives here and now.

Obviously that does not mean that the so-called "far out" projects cannot be materialized, ones much "farther-out" than any presently conceived, in man's own time. Just like books are written a line and a page at a time and motion picture films are made a frame at a time, so are some of man's most ambitious and imaginative projects created. Progress may seem slow. It is, in fact, a relay where a runner hands over the baton of his knowledge to the next runner to the next, and so on until the finish line is reached—the finish line in this case meaning the logical conclusion of a particular project.

If you need reassurance that thoughts are things, the blueprints of your reality, just stop and think about the things you have materialized in your own life. Not one of them could have happened without a preconception, a forethought.

You must bring yourself to believe that, if you are to effect a healing. You must discipline your mind to hold to the positive images so you can be certain those are the ones that your subconscious will act upon.

There is no other way.

When Jesus said to Thomas (John 14:6) "I am the way, the truth and the life . . ." he was simply repeating what He had said over and over again, that for those who believe, nothing is impossible. Nothing is denied.

You must believe with as much conviction in the good things as you believe in the negative thoughts that are responsible for the unpleasant things that happen.

If you are tempted to blame the bad things on outside influences, you must remember that you brought on the negative effects by your own attitudes and prejudices.

Nobody can put a "pox on your house" unless you believe they can! Even if somebody says he or she hates you and wishes you ill health, even death, you may be certain that the damage will be done to the hater, not to the one hated. Hatred is always reflexive. While it might burn up excess adrenaline in the one who hates, it has no power on the object of the hatred unless the hated person fears that it may have.

One of the negative aspects of voodoo is the power given to the shaman or witch doctor by the followers. The healing works and the "black magic" works for exactly the same reason, because the members of the sect or society believe absolutely that it will be effective.

Pins stuck in a doll-like effigy will cause a victim to sicken and die, and horrible tasting potions will cure a person. Why? Not because the shaman is invested with an exclusive power but because the victim or the patient believes he is.

So much for the pitfalls one can blunder into because of a lack of understanding of how the principle works.

Instead, let's spend a few minutes on specific approaches to mental healings that are effected by the remarkable and absolutely dependable power of the subconscious.

It is useless to make a catalogue of incantations or prayers directed against specific diseases. This book would be encyclopedic in length. All that is necessary is to understand the truth in the statements made earlier—*the thrust of the subconscious mind is toward perfect health.*

When you communicate with your subconscious, it is correct to "name" your ailment. *But do not visualize it in detail for then you are giving it negative reality.* "See" yourself as whole. "See" yourself in perfect health. *Imagine* yourself—*visualize* yourself—as well and happy. Remember yourself as you were when you enjoyed your great good health. Recall how well you felt, how much energy you had, how much enthusiasm for living, what wonderful plans you had, what great outings and other recreations you enjoyed without physical limitations.

In short, reinforce the positive things that were once a reality in your life. They still can be. They are not now because you took them for granted and did not take time to think about them and thank the Infinite Spirit for such blessings.

Instead, you allowed negative thoughts to creep in. You began to believe them. It is part of human perversity that we respond more readily to threats than to blessings.

If a friend walks up and says, "You look wonderful today. God bless You!" you'll probably smile and murmur, "Thanks."

If another well-meaning friend walks up, peers at you with worried eyes and says, "You don't look so well today," you'll grow alarmed, lift your hand to your face and breathe, "Oh . . .?" If the friend persists and says, "Yes, you look pale," you'll feel a sharp stab of anxiety and reply, "Really? You mean I look sick?" Right then and there you will begin programming your sub-conscious to manifest some sort of an illness.

Instead of blessing the friend who blessed you, who took the time to compliment you and make you feel good about yourself, you fluffed off the positive input with a simple, "Thanks," and went on about your good business.

But not the negative observation about your health! That really went home!

Why?

Because threats imply an end to our security and well being. We all want to survive. If we feel threatened, then our survival is in question. Suddenly we are "all ears."

There's a "down country" story that makes the point: A Missouri farmer bought a new mule. The animal would not stand still for harnessing. In desperation the farmer called in a neighbor who was known as a good mule skinner. The neighbor studied the mule for a time, then turned to the farmer. "You got a short piece of two by four?" "I reckon so," the farmer replied.

A few minutes later he was back with it.

The mule skinner took out his "toad stabber" and whittled a handle on one end. Then he approached the skittish mule and stared it in the eye for a moment.

Suddenly he hauled off and hit the animal a stunning blow between the ears. The mule's eyes glazed and its knees buckled.

"Why, in the name of all git out did ya do that?" the farmer cried.

"It's very simple," the mule skinner replied. "The first thing you gotta do is git his attention."

Those friends who tell us how poorly we look "git our attention" all right! But it's well to remember that you never have to haul off and smack your subconscious to get its attention. *It is always paying attention, even to the least of our thoughts.*

Earlier we indicated that too often we tend not to believe something if it seems too simple, that an idea to be worth our attention must be complicated, that its value must be in direct proportion to its obscurity.

"Mysterious are the workings of God."

On the contrary. In our lives the workings of God are the very soul of simplicity. That is what every great teacher has taught from the beginning. It is those who have interpreted those original teachings who have most often complicated them, quite possibly to add to their own stature as "wise" men, or women.

You do not have to wait until "the stars are right" or for any other set of conditions before you begin to change your life through your subconscious mind's reaction to your beliefs.

In *The Nature of Personal Reality,** a Seth Book by Jane Roberts, Seth repeats time and again that *"the point of power is the present."*

That means, quite simply, that you can begin to use the power of your subconscious the instant you decide to. There is no "operational delay."

You can choose at this very instant whether your subconscious mind is to be your best friend or your worst enemy. The decision is up to you. The result is inevitable!

*Englewood Cliffs, NJ: Prentice-Hall, 1974.

10

Imaginology
and Creative Talent

*Every person on earth
is creative. There is no such thing
as a non-creative person.
Believe that
profound truth and open an exciting
new door to a fuller, richer life.*

There is not a soul on earth who does not feel the urge to create something that is uniquely personal and original. From earliest childhood we all feel impelled to create something.

What parent hasn't viewed with horror the crayon tracks left on wallpaper by some pint-sized Picasso or the mud pie sculptures on the front steps patted and pushed by loving little fingers into some childish abstraction by a mini-Michaelangelo?

Inherent in all of us is the desire to express ourselves "artistically" in one medium or another. Sometimes a particular talent will be recognized very early in life. Chopin, Mozart, Mendelsohn, Menuhin, Rubenstein—all were child prodigies.

Most of the great painters had childhood compulsions to create graphically. Nearly all of the great ballet dancers showed a special aptitude early in life. Many writers gave promise of being storytellers long before they had mastered the intricacies of the written word.

Imagination in its endless forms began expressing itself in these and other creations. The budding scientist took things apart to see how they worked. The young architect and the youthful engineer designed and constructed things.

The toy companies have long recognized the talent latent in our tots and have, in many cases, done whole generations a splendid service by providing games that stimulate this inborn creativity. Now, in this marvelous age of electronics and mini-computers we can only guess at the creative stimuli that will be available to future generations of our children and young people. Already, in many schools, learning is being accelerated by special computer programs. Recently, in a computer center that sets aside certain hours for students, I watched upper grade grammar school students and high school students using word processors to turn out letter perfect reports. One group, under the supervision of a teacher, was doing its final examinations on the processor. They accepted these modern miracles as easily as my generation accepted the miracle of the old crystal set!

Sometimes creative talent lies dormant for many years before it finds its expression, often quite unexpectedly. Grandma Moses was such an artist.

At present, lovely, and phenomenally successful Jane Wooster-Scott is being called "The New Grandma Moses" by critics on both coasts. Formerly a journalist and society columnist, Jane pursued in private her need to express herself in paint until her secret hobby was discovered by astounded friends who urged her to "go public." Her shows in New York and Los Angeles have been outstanding successes as scores of important collectors have been adding Wooster-Scott to their collections.

Famed sculptress Gladys Lewis Bush, whose heroic bronze protrait head of Mark Twain is in the permanent collection at the Metropolitan Museum of Art in New York, placed there by the author's youngest daughter, Clara, discovered her extraordinary talent while a semi-invalid confined to her bed.

With the discovery of her ability to create in clay and finally in marble, bronze, and wood, her new energy literally propelled her into one of the richest and most exciting lives imaginable. It was a talent she never suspected.

The subconscious process that produced it must have been going on quietly for years, since she did not feel compelled to putter with modeling clay until she was in her early forties. A year after she quit her bed to study, she found herself in Paris, the protogé of the great French modernist, Charles Despiau.

From there Gladys Lewis Bush went on to create extraordinary works. Unable to have children of her own, she gave birth in bronze and marble to portraits of other people's children and the love and longing she put into her portraits brought tears of gratitude to her clients.

In the end, she left as her legacy over fifty beautiful creations ranging from miniatures to heroic portraits and garden pieces in marble and bronze. Many of these grace some of the most beautiful estates in this country and in Europe.

Her famous marble nude of Mae West received the most flattering critical acclaim all over the world. Just before she died, Mae West told a *Life* reporter that the nude, then gracing her ivory-white grand piano, was the most·precious of her possessions.

Creative talent may assert itself from infancy to old age. The urge may be irresistible in early youth or it may not surface until well into our mature years. One thing is certain, however, we all feel the urge for some creative release.

It need not become more than an avocation, a hobby that brings us tranquility and release from the strains of our professions or our jobs; but whatever its function, you may be certain that you possess the ability to express yourself artistically in some fashion or another.

A man who builds a lovely birdhouse is no less an artist at heart than the man who builds a high-rise condominium. A woman who becomes a famous dress designer is no less an artist in spirit than the rural housewife who wins prizes at the county fair for her original hand-made quilts.

As a very young man sailing in the old pre-union days of filthy tramp steamers in the South Pacific, I spent fascinating hours off watch observing the remarkable artistry of Russian John, a White Russian refugee from the revolution, who had come aboard our ship in Vladivistok as a "work away" fleeing to the freedom of the states.

Russian John spoke no English. He was not a particularly able seaman; but no one I ever sailed with, and there were many, could match his talent for scrimshaw work. He created miniatures of surpassing beauty on bits of ivory or shell that he and others scrounged up for him. For the pittance of my youthful admiration (I was not quite seventeen at the time) he gave me several pieces.

Later, I was forced to sell them ashore in Australia and New Zealand for a pound or two to supplement the starvation wages we received in those "good old days." Quite apart from their beauty, they would be worth a fortune now.

Several years after I had come ashore I stopped in at Stevie's Bar on Market Street in San Francisco. There I ran into an old shipmate, Third Officer Ernst Shultz, who told me that Russian John had died of consumption and that not one piece of his beautiful scrimshaw work had been left to pay for his burial expense.

Few professionals have more well-exercised imaginations than "deep water" sailors. Thus it was that Shultz was "certain" that Russian John had been of the nobility. When I think back on it, there was more than language that separated him from the rest of us in the fo'cas'le. He also possessed a quiet dignity that bespoke fine breeding. If I get around to writing a sequel to my first novel,* a story of those days at sea, I shall try to create a more fitting memorial to this mysterious man and his remarkable talent.

How do you apply Imaginology to discover a latent talent? The process is simple, but it does require a little personal detective work.

Sit down with a sheet of paper and list in the order they occur to you those artistic leanings that interest you.

When you have chosen the one that seems to have the most appeal, take up the pendulum we spoke of in Chapter 7. Follow those directions and ask your subconscious if the latent talent you have chosen is the one you could pursue with the greatest chance of success and satisfaction.

Ask the question simply and clearly and prepare yourself in advance to accept and believe the answer. If you want a back-up choice, ask if a second interest might develop also. But don't "muddy up" your mind and confuse your subconscious by asking for a lot of options. The talent you feel for most strongly is probably the one you will be directed to pursue.

Don't make the mistake that so many are tempted to make. Don't expect, because the advice came from your "mysterious inner self" that your talent has been waiting, full blown, in the wings ready to dazzle the world. Creative talent, like any other activity, must be developed. Yehudi Menuhin did not just pick up his fiddle for the first time and rip off the Hungarian Rhapsody to the bravos of an adoring crowd. There were hours and hours of learning the rudiments of the instrument, of polishing technique before he was ready to make his concert debut.

*The Run For Home, New York: Doubleday, 1958.

Gladys Lewis Bush's first pieces of portrait sculpture were remarkable for an untutored beginner but she did not achieve the greatness that finally was hers until she had thrown away or reworked countless attempts at perfection.

The old homily, "You get out of a job what you put in it," can be paraphrased in two ways: "You get out of your talent what you put in it," or "You get out of life what you put in it."

Substitute the word subconscious for life and you've said it all.

Some years ago when I did the first book on retirement called *The Retirement Trap,** one thing became very clear as the research progressed; every man and woman who had pulled out of the mainstream of life needed some creative outlet.

Such outlets seemed to come easier to the women, mainly because they had time enough at last to develop some earlier expressed creative skill. I saw beautifully hand-crafted quilts, sweaters, shawls, tatting and lace; hand-painted china; and quarts of superbly made preserves decorated with original labels. In one roadside shop near Bend, Oregon, I found a treasure-house of cottage-industry crafts made by retired people who had settled in that beautiful part of the state.

Katharine Hepburn, then on location with John Wayne, was similarly entranced. When we both admired a quilt that I wanted very much as a wedding present for my daughter, Allison, that gracious lady deferred to my wishes by pretending an equal interest in another quilt.

The retired men did not seem to find it so easy to uncover latent skills. Most of them said they did not have enough time during the peak years of their professions to do much beyond getting a little exercise. Most of them continued to play golf. Some took up lawn bowling or shuffleboard. In the main, none of those activities satisfied them. "My game's a little better now," one man said, "but you can't spend your life out there on the greens."

A surprising number of men did take advantage of adult education courses, and a great number of those men who had moved to senior citizen communities whose facilites included workshops equipped with the tools needed took up lapidary work, jewelry making, and simple carpentry. A good many of

*New York: Doubleday & Company, 1965.

them also attended drawing classes and beginners' classes in sculpture, oil painting, and water coloring.

Many of them discovered unsuspected talents and created some really fine works.

"Gives me a new lease on life," said one enthusiastic retired vice-president of a large construction company. "Until I discovered I could cut and polish stones and make pretty things with them, I used to go stand around watching new construction jobs and thinking about how much better I could have done it if they hadn't made me retire." He shook his head and shrugged. "Hell, man." he added, "I'm not finished at sixty-five. I'm just beginning to live. Two of my things won prizes and got photographed in a national gem magazine."

Perhaps most of those who belatedly discovered a creative talent did not feel as much satisfacton or receive so much welcome recognition, but most of them confessed to being a lot happier for having discovered they could really create something original. One woman who knitted beautifully told me she was making over two-hundred dollars a month selling her things to a smart shop in a nearby shopping center.

Another woman who crocheted and often sold, said, "It's perfect. I can even watch *General Hospital* and never drop a stitch!"

Two former executives of department store chains decided to organize and manage a swap meet. Their merchandising skills perfectly complemented their new careers.

"It's a good solution," one of them said. "The meets are held on Saturdays. It takes us a couple of hours a day to coordinate them and the rest of the time we have off to spend with our wives, and kids, and grandchildren. By this time next year we will have added about fifty percent to our retirement pay and social security. We can live very well."

In each case these activities provided a service, so a ready market was found. A viable market is no discriminator against age groups. Ask any enterprising kids who set up a homemade lemonade stand on a hot summer day!

Think about the things that appeal to you, the creative arts-

and-crafts-sort-of-things that you have always admired and wished you could do.

Make a list and see which choice makes the brightest light—"turns you on," as the young ones say. Then, ask your subconscious for an opinion. You'll get a "swinging yes" from your pendulum if you've asked the question sincerely, for then your subconscious will know your interest is not superficial.

11

Imaginology and Your Life Partner

Don't sentence your spouse
to complaints of "home imprisonment"
or to endless "reruns" and "instant replays"
of your hard day at the office.
No person really lives a full,
happy life without
a sharing, caring partner.

$\mathbf{H}$e's my good husband and my good friend . . ."

"She's a lot more than my good wife. She's my good friend, too!"

"He's all that and more—a good provider, a good lover and a perfect father."

Far more often than the divorce statistics would seem to indicate, those compliments were voiced by husbands and wives who had made good lives together. Though they gave the lie to the cynics, it is nevertheless true that no other social institution has been so praised and so maligned.

In 1590 the English satirist, John Lyly, wrote, "Marriages are made in heaven and consummated on earth."

Menander, who was born around 342 B.C., went on record as saying, "Marriage, if one will face the truth, is an evil—but a necessary evil."

John Selden wrote, in 1689, "Marriage is a desperate thing."

In her "Essay on Marriage" written in 1935, Marianne Moore wrote, "I wonder what Adam and Eve think of it [marriage] by this time?"

Ambrose Bierce, one of San Francisco's preeminent journalists, wrote just before his mysterious disappearance in 1913, "Marriage is a community consisting of a master, a mistress, and two slaves, making in all, two."

Perhaps the most perceptive observation was made by Shakespeare in *Henry VI.* "A hasty marriage seldom proveth well."

His contemporary, John Donne, said it best of all in his "Twelfth Devotion," from which Ernest Hemingway took the title of what many feel was his greatest work. Donne wrote, "No man is an island, entire of itself; every man is a piece of the continent, a part of the main; if a clod be washed away by the sea, Europe is the less, as well as if a promontory were, as well as if a manor of thy friends, or of thine own were; any man's death diminishes me, because I am involved in mankind; and therefore never send to know for whom the bell tolls; it tolls for thee."

What the sixteenth century metaphysical poet was implying was the tragic waste, the very personal loss in the erosion of the whole. "Man" was the collective noun that included both sexes. The joining together of two people in mutual trust and devotion creates a "continent" of positive being that increases with the being if it is not eroded by the "tides of selfishness and inconsideration."

In this day when nearly half of all marriages in the United States end in divorce, Donne's observation holds special meaning. After some decades of observation, and more than a little practical experience, it seems to me that marriages are really made on earth with Heaven's help.

Be that as it may, the all-too-common male chauvinistic attitude toward marriage quite probably has endured for millenia. There are as many explanations for it as there are philosophers to ponder the problem.

One of the most interesting theories holds that man was unconsciously jealous of woman's mysterious power to create new life within her body. He felt inferior and sought to prove his superiority by saying, "She can't conceive a child without me! More than that, I am the provider, the protector. I am stronger and braver . . ."

That ancient "put-down" gained currency as man convinced himself that his attitude was justified by his domestic lifestyle. After all, he had no periodic inconveniences that deprived him of his marital rights. No other female that he could observe in the animal kingdom suffered such a handicap. Only *his* woman. Obviously, he was superior in many important ways, whereas his mate was confined to the cave, the hut, or the home by physiological and economic necessity. She was dependent. Therefore, she was inferior.

In this era of equal rights, woman still finds herself frustrated, often at the mercy of custom and convention. But, as modern conveniences and education give her more free time to assert her individuality and develop her talents, she is, at long last, "gaining on it."

The old saw, "All men are created equal but some are more equal than others," is losing its spurious credibility. Women are becoming equal partners—equal in importance to each other and to the community of man.

Hasty marriages are usually consummated for very limited reasons. Strong physical attraction is one. To insure one's security is another. To better one's social position is still another. All of these reasons are usually rationalized in the name of "romantic love."

Ludwig Bemelmans once captioned a cartoon this way: "I love you, I love you, I love you. There! I talked myself into it!"

If love requires that much self-hypnosis for consummation, surely it is doomed. We observed that, realistically, marriages are made on earth with Heaven's help. That is just another way of applying the principle of Imaginology, of asking our subconscious to guide us in our decision.

Where love is the concern, it is probably the toughest assignment we can give that loyal, unquestioning part of ourselves.

The pull of physical attraction is second only to the compulsion to survive. The first has to do with the survival of the race. The second concerns the survival of the individual. For some species polygamy relieves most of the sexual pressure. But man, by convention if not by nature, is most frequently monogamous. When convention and compulsion find themselves on a collision course, society trembles.

What we must do in our society is accept the reality of its mores and believe absolutely that it is possible, within those prescribed boundaries, to find a lifetime partner who will balance out those qualities needed to insure a full, happy, healthy, and prosperous life for both.

Since, in our society, it is the only acceptable way we can be fulfilled as individuals, we must turn to our subconscious to help us find the best possible partner.

How much anguish might have been spared had that principle been generally understood! What then do we say to our subconscious mind when we charge it with the responsibility of bringing into our lives the perfect mate?

Again, we turn to a list because it helps us to remember and clarify our thoughts. Set down on the list those qualities you desire in a person.

Do not set down on the list anything that you are unwilling to bring to the union yourself. You are asking for guidance in finding an *equal* partner. Among the attributes should be the following:

Honesty
Sincerity
Loyalty
Affection
Faithfulness
Intelligence
Humor
Industriousness
Creative imagination
Spirituality

Does that sound like an impossible "shopping list"? Not at all. Most successful marriage partnerships, and there are tens of millions of them, partake of each of those qualities.

Not one attribute on this list is difficult to achieve. Try removing one of them from the qualities you want in your partner.

Will you settle for lack of honesty?
Lack of sincerity?
Disloyalty?
Promiscuousness?
Lack of affection?
Stupidity?
Lack of humor? (A lifesaving grace in troubled times!)
Inflexibility?
Slothfulness?
Dull literalness?

Unrelieved materialism?

To compromise with any one of those qualities is to invite dissatisfaction which, before long, will dim the rosy glow of your romance and erode the foundation of your relationship. No two people get together and live their lives out in perfect harmony. Discords are inevitable. Humor and the ability to compromise fairly and willingly are the key to getting the marriage or the partnership back to perfect pitch.

Edmund Burke said, ". . . every human benefit and enjoyment, every virtue and every prudent act—is founded on compromise . . ."

Even so, not all compromise is comfortable or even desirable. One-sided compromise is just another form of surrender. Surrender is the mother of resentment. Resentment is a slow and deadly emotional poison. True compromise is a sincerely accepted, rational reconciliation of differences with which both parties can live comfortably.

Some of the qualities on your list are not susceptible to compromise. Neither can they be demanded if they are not present. Honesty, for instance—and loyalty. That is why, in asking for guidance from your subconscious, you must have a clear picture of the partner you want and believe implicitly that such a person exists now and will be brought into your life.

So, having made a list that you honestly believe will satisfy your physical and emotional needs, find a comfortable place, close your eyes and relax and address your subconscious clearly and sincerely in words such as these:

> What I want most is a compatible mate to share this wonderful gift of life. I want a man [or a woman] to whom I can reach out, to whom I can give the best in me, and whom I can embrace with deepest affection and respect.
>
> I know such a person exists now and is known to you. I ask you to lead us to each other so that we may instantly recognize each other as divinely led to share our lives.
>
> I will ask nothing that I am not prepared to give in return with all of my heart. Among those qualities are Faithfulness, Ambition, Intelligence, Truth, and Humor.

(The first letters of each of those qualities when placed together to form a word spell, FAITH.)

> Faith, ambition, intelligence, truth, and humor—these are the qualities that I will do my best to bring to my mate with all of the strength and determination in me. I make this a solemn pledge to you, my subconscious mind. So be it!

There are a number of ways that one can address the subconscious with such a request. The precise words are not important so long as the request is clear, not ambiguous. Remember, your subconscious is absolutely literal in its interpretations of your requests.

The intensity of the words and the depth of your belief in them are of overriding importance.

You may say, with the devoutness of prayer:

> My deepest desire is to be led to the man [woman] who will bring out and nurture the best in me. I know such a mate lives now and desires the same in his [her] life as deeply as I do. This ideal mate is known to you now. I ask that we be led to each other. I ask with complete faith that it will be so.

Not long ago I talked to a lovely woman of remarkable beauty and candor who only recently had found the man she should have married twenty years earlier.

"I didn't deserve to find the right man then," she said. "I was desperately trying to get away from my small town and the memory of the first man I loved, who was killed in an accident.

"I don't know that he would have been the best man for me either. But I do know that I loved him and I would have given him the best in me. That was not destined to be. What I got was what I deserved, what I was really asking for, a man who would take care of me and get me out of the confines of my little town and the unhappiness it represented.

"Now that I understand the principle of Imaginology I realize that my subconscious brought me exactly what I had been asking for without questioning the wisdom of my choice. The man I married had been sent to our town to help establish a branch of a national company. He was very attractive, the most eligible man around. Every single girl in town, and some who weren't single, set their caps for him.

"I was very attractive then—nineteen, with all of the assets of youth, a provocative body, energy, love of fun, and a good sense of humor. It was not difficult to beat out the other girls. My father said, 'You made him chase you until you caught him!'"

The woman, still lovely in every way and the mother of two teenagers, a boy and a girl, cocked her head thoughtfully.

"I don't think we'd been married more than a month when misgivings began to set in. I knew I'd made a mistake. I wanted to do something about it but I was afraid of the censure and ridicule I was certain to receive. I had been a young, impulsive fool. More than that, I was stubborn. I was determined not to admit that I had made a mistake.

"When I found out I was pregnant I knew I had to stick it out. We moved five times in four years as my husband's work took him from city to city, and finally, country to country, to establish new branches.

"Unexpectedly, I got pregnant again. I had little or no economic security. I was afraid to try to make it alone. When my daughter was born I knew the children had to stay with me.

"Would you believe, it took me twenty years to get up enough gumption and faith in myself to stand alone and care for my kids? I told myself that I wanted to wait until the children were older and could be on their own a bit more. That was really not the truth. I was just plain scared stiff! I had never worked. I did not know what I could do."

Finally, this lovely woman separated from her traveling husband and found a job. She told me about those first terrifying weeks and how a friend of hers who understood the principles of Imaginology took her to a lecture. She was a waitress at the time.

"It was the turning point of my life," she said. "I did not know that I had a talent for selling but I did know that it was easy for me to meet people. I like them. And I did know that I loved art in all of its forms. Very soon I found a job as a gallery representative and immediately I knew that I had found my place.

"It was rough going at times. We were divorced and I asked for no alimony, only a very modest sum for child support. My husband had lost his job and could not contribute a dime but, somehow, with my salary and commissions, I was able to get by. My son helped with odd jobs after school and my daughter found time to babysit and study.

"For the first time in my life I felt free and independent. I was told not to feel guilty about my unhappy marriage. I was told to forgive myself and get on with my life, secure in the knowledge that the right man for me would come along, a man to whom I would be deeply attracted, a man who would welcome the chance to share all of the best things in me that I was longing to give."

Did this lovely lady find her ideal man—and how long did it take?

"During the first year," she continued, "I met several men, mostly divorced, who I thought attracted me. But when it came to making a decision I found myself being tempted to marry again for the wrong reasons—for security—for someone to assume the responsibility of caring for me and my children—someone to take the pressure off.

"Each time that happened I caught myself and went back to reaffirm my faith that the subconscious mind would bring me the man I really wanted, for all the right reasons. I practiced patience—not easy for me—and kept my vision clear. And then one day, when I was looking my absolute worst, it happened!

"I had changed from the chic dress I wore in the gallery to an old dress and apron. I had a bandeau tied around my hair and I was pushing the vacuum cleaner around the studio a half hour before opening.

"I had forgotten to relock the front door and suddenly it opened and there he was, a nice looking man wearing a quizzical smile.

"I gaped at him and finally got the wheezing old vacuum cleaner turned off. I could see perspiration glistening on my nose and feel it on my forehead. I dabbed at it with the back of my hand and finally managed to say, 'I'm not open . . .

"The man's generous mouth widened into a broad grin.

"'I'm sorry to hear that,' he said.

"'I mean, the gallery's not open,' I blurted, then felt like a .fool. This time he laughed outright. It was the merriest sound I'd heard in ages.

"'Suppose I go across the way for some coffee and come back later? Would a half hour be enough time?'

"'Oh, yes,' I assured him. 'We open at nine. I could even open a little earlier if it would help.'

"He glanced at his watch. 'That's only twenty minutes from now. Time for a coffee.' He started to leave and paused in the doorway. 'Why don't I bring back one for you? Do you take cream and sugar?'

"'Well—I—uh—just black, thank you.'

"When he had gone I found myself as nervous as a girl at her first prom. For some reason the stranger seemed familiar. A lot of people come through the gallery. I felt certain I would not have forgotten this man with his wonderful smile and still I did not recall having seen him before.

"I gave the rest of the place a lick and a promise and hurried in the back to change. Thank heaven I'm still blessed with a face that's easy to put back together!

"When I came out he was standing at the locked door holding two plastic cups of steaming coffee. I let him in quickly and for some reason locked the door behind him.

"He offered me a cup and said, 'I thought I'd have seconds with you while I look around. Do you mind?'

"'Of course not!' I said with more feeling than I had intended.

"He indicated two chairs in a little reception corner. 'I'm in no rush unless you are. Why don't we sit there and have our coffee and I'll tell you what I'm looking for?'"

The woman recounting this—it's hard to believe that she is the mother of a nineteen-year-old son and a sixteen-year-old daughter—certainly is at her most beautiful in her mid-forties, as most women are. Anticipating the outcome, I listened as she continued.

"We have been married for a year now and there's no way I can tell you how much I love that man. He had been married before and has two grown daughters. He adores his daughters and my son and daughter adore him too. He never tries to take their father's place in their affections. As a result they give him the warmest loving appreciation. The mutual respect in this family is one of the greatest blessings of my life.

"Do I believe Imaginology works? You had better believe I do!"

She reached over and took my hand. "I'll never be afraid of anything again," she said in a low, lovely voice, warm with conviction. "I know now that I shall never really be alone, no matter what happens."

When I asked this happy lady how she had communicated with her subconscious mind in order to bring the right man into her life she said, "I just imagined real hard what I wanted him to be, and what I wanted to be to him—faithful, ambitious, intelligent, truthful, and humorous. All of those things and more!

"I did not say he had to be six feet tall with blond hair and blue eyes or that he had to be a second Cary Grant, who was my girlhood idol. I didn't visualize features at all, just the quality of personality that I knew I could love and live with."

As it turned out, the man in her life is six-feet-one inches tall and he does have blue eyes—really blue-gray eyes. In his youth he had blond wavy hair but as he himself says, "There's still some of the original color left, but the hairs are further apart now."

At a time when most men are down-shifting into late middle age, her husband is crackling with energy. He is a professional man but he is also a competent artist, a fine skier, a good swimmer, a dedicated trout fisherman, and a fine horseman, the legacy of his youth on his family's ranch. His radiant wife now keeps up with him joyfully through most of his activities and fairly bubbles with the excitement of living.

The point to remember is this: Her story is not the exception; it is the rule—if the rules of Imaginology are followed.

You must have a clear concept—a clear vision—of what you want and, more than that, an honest reason for wanting it.

Do not set a time limit on what you want. Curb your impatience as she did and certainly curb your anxiety. Both are negatives that will block the manifestation of the things you wish for.

So, Imaginology, the art and science of programming your infallible subconscious to bring into your life those good things you desire and need, can work for young people seeking a perfect life partner, for people in their middle years who want another chance, and for older people who wish to live out their life spans fully and productively.

After a lecture at a senior citizen community, a lady in her seventies came up to the platform leading a gentleman who was obviously her contemporary.

"You know," she said with a happy smile, "we hear so often that when we reach a certain age we should give up hope of finding happiness again if we are left alone." She pulled the man closer to her side. "This is Tom. He and my late husband worked together in Detroit for years. I came out here five years ago when I couldn't take the cold anymore. Tom came out here a year ago when he was left alone."

Her eyes shone. "It's wonderful!" she exclaimed. "We have so many things in common from the old days at G.M."

Tom, a sturdy, distinguished-appearing man with white hair and an easy smile, nodded in agreement. "It's almost as if fate took a hand," he said, "finding Madge here. It's a whole new life."

When I asked if either of them had abandoned hope, both of them denied it emphatically.

"When I was first left alone," Tom said, "I admit to a lost feeling. I knew I couldn't bring Edna back, and I knew she would not want me to live out my life alone, so I just gathered myself together and got going again. It worked!"

The woman called Madge locked her arm through his and nodded. "My motto has always been, 'While there's life there's hope!' I don't know who said it first but it's true."

Tom added a fervent, "Amen!"

I couldn't help but smile as I remembered a sign I had seen at the gate of a retirement community in Arizona. Some wag had painted it on cardboard and propped it against the post. It read, "All hope abandon, ye who enter here."

As I watched Tom and Madge go up the aisle toward the exits I felt a deep sense of satisfaction that the grim humorist who had borrowed the ironic line from Dante's Inferno, had been wrong . . . and in Cicero's hopeful line, *"Dum anima est, spes est,"* nothing had been lost in Madge's translation!

We must add "Amen" to that too, for hope and belief are the handmaidens of our happy tomorrows.

Hope is never negative unless we say, "I hope it happens," but in our hearts we doubt that it will. Those are called forlorn hopes. Don't waste your time on them.

Hope for what you want in life, for anything good that you want, *and believe that it will happen.*

Your subconscious will then get a clear, positive image and a command that it must obey.

12

Imaginology
and Heredity

*Don't hang yourself
on your family tree.*

We go back to scriptural quotations from time to time, not so much because they carry the special significance of sacredness but because of their obvious logic and common sense.

In Ecclesiastes, 30:14–16, we are reminded that "*there is (sic) no riches above a sound body.*"

Who would contradict that statement? How many of us have known rich men and women who suffer miserably from poor health? And who among them would not trade their riches for perfect health?

Fortunes have been and are still being spent to regain that blessing of blessings.

Someone, questioning the power of the subconscious, is certain to ask, "But what about those poor souls who were born with infirmities—weak organs, malformed limbs, faulty speech, faulty hearing and eyesight and a score of other physical defects?"

If we listen to our doctors and physiologists, we are told that these tragic misfortunes are the result of genetic aberrations,—inherited irregularities in the genetic chain—or birth damage.

It is difficult to refute that argument. These scientists have accumulated convincing evidence in their laboratories. Often these afflictions are called genetic accidents.

Defective offspring can come from apparently normal parents. When that occurs the geneticists go back several generations to investigate grandparents and great-grandparents. Sometimes the evidence they seek seems not to exist, or it has been lost.

On the other hand, the metaphysicians, the mystics and the mediums, and a great many once skeptical investigators who are interested in the supernatural or the paranormal have become convinced by the evidence that the largely nonreversible defects were predestined before conception.

Those unfortunate victims are thought to be souls who deliberately chose to experience a grave physical handicap in order to deepen their understanding of the earthly experience or to make amends for transgressions committed in a past life.

Such psychical handicaps have been labeled Karma, old debts accumulated in past lives that must be settled, old lessons not learned that must be learned in a present incarnation for the further refinement of the soul.

These are two radically divergent points of view. One is conventionally scientific and the other has been labeled, "pseudo-scientific nonsense" or "just plain bunk."

It is not the purpose here to expose or expound either point of view. Over the centuries a lot of misinformation has been given the respectability of scientific confirmation until further research proved it to be fallacious.

By the same token, the metaphysical point of view has remained under question despite the fact that a number of respected scientists with adventurous minds have applied the techniques of disciplined research and investigation to the theory of reincarnation and received the surprise of their academic lives.

In the light of what we do know about Imaginology, the working of the subconscious mind, there are some unquestionable facts from which we may draw hope and comfort.

Dramatic spiritual healings can and do happen, regularly.

Some physical defects can be repaired by modern medical science and, at the same time, many physical infirmities can be healed by the subconscious process.

Holistic medicine uses both methods.

When an orthodox medical practitioner says, "Your theory is simply a panacea, a cure-all, a 'mental patent medicine' that has no validity," there is one question that must be asked: "How does it happen that, after months and years of research, a scientist suddenly gets an inspiration and tries something entirely new to solve a problem and, miraculously, he is successful?" He has pursued all of the conventional research procedures. All of the logical sequences have been explored to no effect. Then, suddenly, he departs from the logical, "tried and true" methods, responds to an intuitive hunch, and, wonder of wonders, there it is!

Where did the intuitive idea come from?

It came from his subconscious mind as a result of his deep conviction and dedication to the solution, a result that he never really doubted he'd find! Unqualified belief again. The inevitable result of the synergistic interaction of the I.B.M. "formula."

The physicians and surgeons—and no one will dispute their genius—can and do perform their own miraculous healings regularly. Most of them will agree that the mental attitude, the faith, of the patient has a great deal to do with the success of the treatment.

I have talked to a number of physicians who have seen complete remissions in patients whose illnesses have been diagnosed as terminal. Most of them could find no explanation if there was no obvious misdiagnosis.

Some will ascribe such miracles to the completion of a karmic debt. They will say that the pain, the anxiety, and, finally, the faith in the physician was all the soul needed to experience. The subconscious had done its job.

How often have we heard someone say, "I think I inherited my father's weak lungs," or "I inherited my mother's bad back," or "I inherited my grandfather's talent for mathematics," or "My daughter inherited my love of music," or "She inherited my mother's wonderful complexion"?

In claiming those inheritances we regard as unfortunate, as negative, we are unconsciously excusing in ourselves some imagined shortcoming or limitation. "It is not my fault," we say to ourselves, "that I have this problem. I inherited it."

Most often such a statement is a self-serving "cop out."

We know that we cannot grow new limbs yet, or new livers, or new eyes or teeth. Neither can we grow new hearts or lungs. Perhaps one day the genetic engineers will figure out how to do those things and, like some reptiles, we'll be able to grow some selective new parts. If that happens, it will be because those scientists believed without question in their ability to solve the riddle, and the subconscious mind, responding to their belief, will have led them to the right answers.

All of us seem to inherit qualities, appearances, traits, and talents. Moreover, we assume that we have inherited them from some forebear who was similarly blessed or disadvantaged.

Cloning notwithstanding, genetic engineers cannot say that a certain arrangement of genes will produce a violin virtuoso, or a great painter, or a great writer, dancer, philosopher, or industrial tycoon.

They can say that a certain arrangement of genes will produce tall people, short people, dark people, light people, dull people, bright people, and human carbon copies. Those qualities have only to do with physical reproduction.

The talents that made a man like Charles Steinmetz an electrical genius, or Albert Einstein a soaring intellect who could imagine, and later confirm, some of the greatest secrets of the universe; or Leonardo da Vinci a super-genius in art, literature, medicine and engineering; or Albert Schweitzer, a totally unselfish physician and philosopher as well as a talented musician, did not come about as the result of some ideal genetic arrangement. These are qualities of the spirit.

Many may be uncomfortable with the thought, but it seems more likely that our talents, no matter how modest or what the degree of brilliance, are extentions in this life of gifts that were granted in previous lives.

How else can one explain the young Chopin and Mozart and so many other prodigies? How else can one explain a child of three who sits down at the piano without a single lesson and, to the amazement of all, begins to play sonatas? And what of the young lad of seven who can add a string of "box car numbers" in his head as fast as a computer, or the child, never exposed to any language other than that of his parents, who suddenly begins speaking fluently in an archaic tongue, or another who predicts the future with astonishing accuracy, or still another who describes in accurate detail life in the court of an Egyptian ptolemy three centuries before Christ?

Novelist Taylor Caldwell completely flabbergasted medical historians with her knowledge of medical practices in ancient Rome. Without ever having done a lick of research on the subject, she described in absolutely accurate, confirmable detail the ancient procedures used in brain surgery, exploratory laparotomies, amputations, and complicated diagnoses.

When asked how she knew such a wealth of obscure medical lore, she answered simply, "I don't know. I just know it."

None of this material could have been absorbed in her conscious mind by some sort of intellectual osmosis. The only possible explanation for phenomena of this sort is simply that such specialized knowledge must have been carried forward from other lifetimes in the subconscious repositories of those so blessed.

Is it, then, unreasonable to suppose that the talents we feel an urge to express did not originate in our present lives but, rather, were carried forward as a sort of spiritual credit on our life ledgers?

In the face of the evidence how can one say that these "gifted ones" did not come back to continue refining their creative talents so they could share them with us and inspire us to some creative thought of our own. Would these talents not be gifts inherited from the "themselves" they once were?

If we are the sum total of our past lives, and after three decades of study I firmly believe we are, then we have access to riches beyond compare to draw from, and the key to that treasure chest is the subconscious mind.

It cannot be said often enough that the amount of riches we can attract in this lifetime depends entirely on the strength of our faith and on the power of our imaginations.

The methods for accomplishing that is what Imaginology is all about.

It makes no difference what you desire, so long as you desire it with all of your "heart and soul." Then it must come to you. It is an immutable law. It cannot be amended or retracted.

To wish with all of one's heart and soul is not a sort of quaint or "square" way of putting it if you understand what those two words really mean.

"Heart" means your conscious mind.

"Soul" means your subconscious mind.

Those two inseparable parts of you working together are what produce the miracles in your life.

In earlier pages I talked about the part Imaginology plays in our health, in our prosperity, and in our creativity. Implicit in those discussions is the truth that we are much, much more than we appear to be.

There's far, far more to thee and me Than mortal eyes are wont to see. *

If, however, we learn to use our "third eye," our imagination, then, like the title of the Broadway musical hit, *On a Clear Day You Can See Forever,* we'll have unlimited vision too.

What we call intuition, often called insight without rational conscious thought, is spontaneous knowledge received from the subconscious mind. When we are tempted to pluralize it by saying our subconscious minds, we resist the temptation because the subconscious is not parceled in individual packages. It is universal. There is only one subconscious mind and we all tap it. Otherwise, how could it bring into our lives all of those things that come as a result of our faith, our belief?

How could we meet our ideal mate or find the ideal job in places we have not been before, or how could we be guided to develop our most fulfilling talent? It must be clear that a universal subconscious mind does not have to start asking around of other such minds to get answers. It is complete in itself.

It knows all the answers, and all of the solutions, and it knows how they are best applied in our lives. We all have a rich inheritance, then, the richest one possible. We are all a part of the Divine Spirit, the All There Is. We are all "God's Chil'un." We are all an expression of the Divine Whole. We all have access to those inexhaustible riches.

The only thing that can limit us is lack of belief and lack of faith in our eternal right to grow, to be well, to be happy, to express ourselves freely, and to share to the fullest in those universal riches that are stored in the subconscious mind awaiting those who understand how to reach them and use them.

*Leland Frederick Cooley. *Feel Better Book.* (in work)

The subconscious mind is a sort of Divine Public Utility available to all. In this case, *there is no charge for its use other than the penalties we exact from ourselves by misusing its power or failing to use it consciously to illuminate our lives.*

13

Your Imagination

*The non-stop
miracle machine.*

Bertrand Russell said, "It is only through imagination that men can become aware of what the world might be."

Whether you call Imaginology a system or a science, its function is to show us how to use our imaginations to better our world by bettering ourselves.

Science is said to be a branch or department of systematized knowledge that can be made a specific object of study. Imaginology qualifies on that score.

System is said to be the structure, or whole, formed by the essential principles or facts of a science or branch of knowledge. Imaginology meets that criteria also since it is a branch or department of the greater science of mind management which gathers under its commodious umbrella everything to do with the mind from simple memory courses to abstruse psychology.

Earlier you read what some of the great thinkers and achievers have said of imagination. All agreed that it is a powerful force. Like any powerful force, if it is misdirected it can be destructive.

In these pages Imaginology has sought to simplify the rules for handling this all-powerful mental force positively. Your conscious mind is the key. Unless it is disciplined it can become an aimless wanderer, turning here, turning there, reacting to endless unrelated stimuli, leading you in circles.

Earlier we discussed the barrage of negative thought that is continually being directed at us through the media. We are affected by it both consciously and subliminally. Our subconscious mind is affected. It can begin to feed back into our personal experience feelings of unrest and fears, emotions that lurk just below the threshold of our conscious awareness.

In the practice of Imaginology, that possibility is one of the principal things we must guard against. To do that, it is necessary to recognize the threat and realize that negative ideas have no power over our lives unless we grant them such power by believing they do.

We don't have to be sick because we are told we may be. We don't have to have accidents because we are told we are likely to. We don't have to lose our shirts in these "hard times" because we have not invested in gold or silver or diamonds.

Imagination is like a coin. It has two sides or faces. One side we call, "heads." The flip side we call, "tails." If we manage our imaginations so they come up heads, which means simply that we are using our heads to control our thoughts, we shall be certain winners.

If our thoughts come up tails, we shall surely put our tails between our legs and retreat into trouble and despair. If that happens, we'll discover that we cannot escape from our problems until we have finally come to realize that they are the materialization of undisciplined negative thoughts.

When we come to that realization we can flip our conscious minds over to "positive" and we'll find ourselves in a "heads up" configuration, to paraphrase our Astronauts' lingo.

We must understand, however, the paradoxical nature of the conscious mind. The thoughts we generate in it are both the motor and the vehicle of our imaginations. We conceive something we want and give it the power needed to move it into being, solely through thoughts initiated in the conscious mind. The subconscious mind goes along for the trip without ever asking our destination.

With our conscious minds we can, if we wish, build purely imaginary worlds. In the chapter on creativity we saw how artists and writers and musicians create such worlds.

With the subconscious mind we create reality, but the first concept begins with our ability to imagine or visualize what we wish it to manifest or materialize. The reality of the imaginary things the artist creates is in the book or the painting or the composition that results. The purpose was not to actualize the fantasy or the imaginary creation but to produce a material likeness of it in the medium of choice.

When the great Italian writer, Dante Alighieri, wrote *The Divine Comedy* in the fourteenth century his conscious mind propelled his imagination into one of the immortal pieces of literature.

Dante did not use his imagination to create an Inferno, an unspeakable Hell-on-Earth to which tormented souls were consigned. It is probably true that he believed, as did so many people back then (and still do), in the reality of a heaven and hell apart from earth. That was not his purpose. His purpose was to create an allegory and that he did magnificently.

The best possible reason for learning to use the principle of Imaginology is to prevent us from creating our own imaginary hells on earth by allowing our conscious minds to keep coming up "tails," to keep from being occupied with negative thoughts that block out the possibility of health, wealth, achievement of any positive sort, and our ultimate goal, happiness.

Earlier in these pages you were asked to demonstrate for yourself how your thoughts affect your emotions. You did this by recalling (imagining) the saddest day in your life and the happiest day.

The results were a clear example of the law of cause and effect. Put your food on the fire, the fire will cook it. Put your finger in that same flame and the flame will burn it. The flame has no choice, no responsibility beyond doing your bidding, but, simplistic as it may seem, any flame improperly used or improperly attended can quite literally burn your house down!

Every time you allow your imagination to visualize trouble, illness, and disaster you have no choice. Your subconscious will *cause* those *effects* to appear in your life.

Every time you consciously control your imagination and direct it to see, to visualize, good health, freedom from want, the joy of achievement, the blessings of unselfish love, and the happiness that proceeds from these positive conditions that must then materialize in your life, you are making the law of cause and effect work for you. You are making yourself and your loved ones better. You are making the world better.

Again, you must believe. Always, you must believe in the operation of the principle of Imaginology with the same faith you have in the law of gravity.

The strength of your belief determines the strength of the subconscious power, and it controls the speed and the completeness of your subconscious creations. There are no exceptions. All of us allow our conscious minds to slip the leash now and then. We do this, not because we are the "poor damned souls" we have been accused of being, but because we are simply mortal and, in spite of ourselves at times, we make mortal "mistakes."

We are here to learn. Seth confirms this through medium-author Jane Roberts in the book, *The Nature of Personal Reality*, by saying, in part, ". . . you are here to learn the ways of creativity as directed through conscious thought."

To imagine. To visualize. To "see with the mind's eye." To conceive. One and the same—the process of making "mental pictures."

How many times have you heard someone say, "Picture in your mind if you will . . ."?

We do it all the time. Imaginology is not asking you to learn something you don't know. *You do know how to imagine, how to "picture in your mind . . ."*

What housewife, while redecorating her home, has not stood back and pictured in her mind how the new drapes should look? Soon she has a vivid mental picture of those drapes hanging in place. Soon after that, with complete faith that she'll find them, she heads for the shopping mall, rummages around for a while, and there they are. She may have seen them on sale in the paper, in which case her prayer has been answered sooner! Or, she may go to the store "knowing" that she'll find just the right thing. The principle is the same.

To "know" that the right job, the right person, the right decision will be found is exactly the same principle at work again. You just have to *believe* that any of the other things you want in your life are as accessible as those drapes! All you must do is visualize them as clearly.

We could have called Imaginology by another name—Visiology, for instance, or Conceptology, but we chose Imaginology because imagine is a comfortable word. We understand it. Most of us, however, have not understood the enormous power latent in the act of imagining something when it is accompanied by absolute faith or belief. How foolish, then, not to learn to use that power.

Around 50 A.D. Seneca deplored man's fallibility when he said, "What fools these mortals be!"

Sixteen hundred years later Shakespeare, who apparently only cribbed from the best, wrote in *A Midsummer Night's Dream*, "Lord, what fools these mortals be!"

The fools they referred to, most likely, were we "ordinary mortals" who are sometimes blind to the obvious truth. Imaginology's whole purpose is to open our eyes, to show us how, by making some simple changes in the way we think, we can ask our subconscious mind to set aside the defective lumber we have been using to build our lives and substitute instead the top-grade material needed for a lasting and secure life structure.

The key is imagination, but we must put some practical restraints on it until we have learned how to take two steps forward without taking one back. The restraint is to continually mind our conscious thoughts.

There's a much repeated story that is apropos—about the Australian aborigine who killed himself trying to throw away his old boomerang.

We have to be very careful when we try to "throw away" our old negative thought patterns that they do not boomerang on us by sneaking back into our consciousness and negating the positive thoughts we seek to substitute in their place.

You can do that by recalling, at the first sign of a negative intrusion, the clear picture you have imagined, and by holding it strongly in mind until the negative idea has been replaced.

Those sneaky negatives are often hangovers from old habit patterns, old ways of thinking. Someone called them "gophers in the garden of our desires." Not bad, for they do gnaw at the roots of our positive thoughts.

A lot of great people who have apparently achieved the pinnacle of *success* have been destroyed at the height of *that* success by the persistent negatives they have been unable or have forgotten to "dig out" of their consciousness.

Young Abe Lincoln, belly-down in front of the fire in that little log cabin in Illinois, poring over his precious books, must have begun his dream that ended in the White House during those long nights.

But somewhere in the recesses of his mind there must have been a deeply held fear or premonition that finally resulted in his assassination at Ford's Theater. More than once he confided to his wife that he had dreamt of a violent end.

Minutes before his own assassination John F. Kennedy is said to have remarked, "If anybody wanted to shoot the president, all he'd have to do would be to hide in one of these tall buildings with a powerful rifle. Nothing could be done about it."

History books are filled with accounts of premonitions that later came true—Alexander the Great, Caesar, Marc Antony, Brutus, Cleopatra, and Socrates too! And the martyrs—all brought about their own ends by refusing to renounce their "heresies."

Unless we hold strongly and clearly to our positive "imaginary blueprints" we invite our own martyrdom at the hands of our own negative convictions.

The subconscious mind never disappoints. It never fails to meet its commitments. Don't ever imagine that it does. It is impossible to run away from your own shadow.

The ability to imagine is the greatest gift the Supreme Being has given us. We humans alone have the ability to reason, to visualize, to imagine. It is a gift almost without limitation.

In the laboratories it has been proven that some animals apparently can reason within certain limitations. Animals with brain capacities most nearly approaching those of human beings seem to be able to reason remarkably well though we will not know exactly how well until we learn to communicate with them. Be that as it may, we are the most generously gifted of all living creatures where reason and imagination are concerned. For us not to use this gift to the fullest is an affront to common sense, if not to life itself.

Given the ability to reason, to visualize, to imagine, we are also endowed with the ability to make our lives anything we wish.

We can wallow in self-pity and negative imaginings, we can say we are underprivileged, that others are luckier than we are, we can suffer the torment of envy, and make invidious comparisons "'til hell freezes over." If we do, we'll have to wait until "hell freezes over" for good things to happen to us—*unless we turn our heads around.*

On the other hand, if we've had enough of pain and mental anguish, enough misfortune and self-doubt, we can give our subconscious mind a clear directive to change things and in so doing we can begin one of the most exciting and rewarding journeys we mortals can take.

Many books spend a lot more time telling us *what* we should do than they spend telling us *how* to do it. This is intended to be a "how to" book. For that reason it should be read and reread, chapter by chapter, since no chapter deals with a condition that is not of prime importance in our lives on this earth, and possibly beyond.

Certainly one chapter that should be reviewed time and time again is Chapter 5, our I.B.M. reminder.

I for Imagine,
B for Believe,
M for Materialize.

That is the creative trilogy, the three-step stairway to all the good things that one could want in a lifetime.

Let's go back to that dreadful four-letter word, Envy, too. Nothing will block our personal progress more surely than to envy someone else's success or good fortune.

In the Ten Commandments the word "covet" is used. The words are interchangeable.

If you covet something your neighbor has, it is because you imagine that thing is better than something you possess, or you are envious because you do not possess it. Because he or she has it, you feel inferior. You have devalued yourself unjustly. You have "put yourself down." By coveting or envying, you have locked yourself into your misfortune. You have sentenced yourself to a feeling of lack and inferiority. What a waste!

There is only one thing to do with envy. *Root the word and the emotion out of your vocabulary and out of your heart.*

Instead, imagine the satisfaction the other person must feel from having demonstrated the positive force of the subconscious. *It is the same subconscious that is a part of you.* Bless his or her good luck, knowing that luck really had no part in it. Call it "luck" if it makes you feel easier, but do so knowing that what we call luck is really only the effect of positive imagining motivated by complete faith in the outcome.

Feel what your friend is feeling. Identify yourself with it. Imagine it and pray for it, not out of a sense of one-upmanship—not to prove that you are just as good—but to prove to yourself that when you consciously and purposely imagine something beneficial and do so with all of your heart and soul, it will be yours, it will materialize in your life just as it did in that of the other person.

Do not mistrust the process because it sounds so simple. Nothing the human being has invented thus far has been as useful as the lever and the wheel. Nothing is basically simpler.

Imaginology is not a "magic formula" for success. Imaginology is just the simplest, most direct way to bring into your life all of the good things that you will deserve if you believe you do.

Remember what Matthew said? "Whatsoever ye shall ask in prayer, believing, ye shall receive." And Mark? "What things soever ye desire, when ye pray, believe that ye receive them and ye shall have them."

How many times do we have to be told that truth before we get up enough gumption to believe in "believing?"

14

Imaginology and the Power of Prayer

*Ask and it shall
be given to you.*

A minister friend said not long ago, "Thank God our young people are beginning to believe in prayer." A moment later he added with a twinkle, "And God thanks them for believing."

God certainly does thank us for believing.

Belief is the power behind all prayer, the power that makes manifest in our lives all of the good things we need and ask for, those good things brought into our lives through the operation of the Universal Mind acting through our subconscious mind.

Unfortunately some people still find themselves uneasy when the Universal Spirit or Universal Mind or Divine Mind or The All There Is is referred to simply as God.

There seems to be little enough self-consciousness with many such persons when they are taking the Lord's name in vain, and there is hardly any self-consciousness when, in a dire emergency, they appeal to God to help them.

But God, as an everyday, ever-present friend, comforter, and companion each step of the way somehow seems to make a great many people uneasy when, in fact, His entire purpose is just the opposite.

One of the reasons seems to be a general skepticism, much of which is understandable. I asked a group of young friends about this and got an enlightening answer. One young man said, "Too many people are running around God-blessing everybody these days. They say it like they say, 'Have a nice day.' They say it without thinking. It's just words, hollow words. There's no sincerity. I don't trust them."

A young woman said, "God blesses me every time I think of Him and how much a part of Him I am. I had an aunt who lived in Moline when I was a kid. She had trained a parrot to say, 'God Bless you, brother, God Bless you, sister,' every time someone came into the room. I think a lot of these God blessers are just like that parrot, repeating words they don't know the meaning of."

There were other comments in a similar vein. They reminded me of a well-known western musical star I once worked with in television. He's gone now, a tragic little man who made Imaginology work for a while for all of the wrong reasons.

The man would sprinkle even the shortest conversations with "God bless ya, son," or "God love ya, sister."

After a time I got vaguely annoyed and asked him why he did it. "People like it," he replied, "and it makes me sound very sincere."

The late Dave Garroway, with whom I had frequent business contact during my Madison Avenue days, often ended a show with a blessing. Usually he just murmured, "Peace," and lifted his hand in a modest benediction.

Unlike many public characters, many of them in show business where effect is important, Dave's benediction was meant with heartfelt sincerity. Nobody who knew that remarkable man could ever have thought otherwise.

In *Huckleberry Finn*, Mark Twain wrote, "You can't pray a lie—I found that out."

When you pray with hollow words or when you pray vindictively for somebody's misfortune you are asking for, and receiving, empty answers, or you are inviting to have visited on you the same misfortune you have prayed to have visited on your enemy.

The principle is clearly stated in Galatians, 6:6, where it is written, "Be not deceived; God is not mocked: For whatsoever a man soweth, that shall he also reap."

Some of the most honest, heartfelt prayer I've ever heard came from the lips of so-called "he men" who professed to feel that praying was "sissy stuff" until they were faced with a life-and-death situation.

One of them, with whom I served during World War II, a former merchant sailor like myself, survived a dangerous ordeal involving a loaded aviation fuel tanker and a Russian ammunition ship.

When the danger passed he looked at me sheepishly and said, "I sure as hell am glad that God was listening! Guess I'll have to keep in touch with Him more."

That statement was a sincere prayer in itself!

I pointed out to him that many a fearless prizefighter said a short prayer in his corner before coming out at the bell to face what, at best, would be some brutal punishment.

In this day of television sports it is a common sight to see a famous baseball player unobtrusively cross himself and ask Heaven's help as he faces his first pitch.

If anyone seriously questions whether or not "he men" pray, they would do well to remember Father Duffy, the immortal Catholic priest with the American Expeditionary Force in France during World War I. He earned the love and admiration of hundreds of doughboys for his bravery under fire and his unselfishness in helping those who needed spiritual comfort in the face of almost certain death.

There is no difference between the principle of Imaginology and prayer. What determines the result is the belief, the fervency with which the prayer is uttered, and the faith that it will be heard and answered.

Prayers do not go to one department and requests to another. There is only one "department" where all of our requests are heard and acted upon and that is our great, God-given subconscious mind, the single spiritual entity that is shared by all.

It makes no difference whether we prostrate ourselves before an alter, kneel down in our pews, sit quietly in an easy chair or at our desks, or relax in bed. It is all the same to the subconscious. It does not say, "You are not showing me the proper respect if you do not get down on your knees."

Some of the most fervent prayers I ever uttered were whispered as I huddled, half-frozen, in the "greenhouse" of a war-weary old B-17 bomber at 13,000 feet in a blinding sleet storm. Two of the four engines were out!

Later, safely on the ground, the crew chief, a veteran of some twenty-five bombing runs over Germany, said, "I've had a lot of practice doing this! I not only prayed to God to get us back, but I thanked the folks at Boeing who built these crates. They keep flying' when the birds are walking!"

So, prayers are not the exclusive privilege of the pious. True piety, like a sneeze, can sometimes come unexpectedly, depending on the situation. When it does, it clears your head. I have no doubt that my shipmate or that crew chief seldom forget the blessings they received in their hour of need.

Prayers are the ultimate form of conscious communication, the one that reaffirms the link between man and his Maker, the one that links man with the source of all life, The Universal Spirit that we call God.

The Universal Spirit, the soul or the subconscious mind, and the conscious mind that defines the individual "you" are all different parts, different manifestations of the One. The conscious mind flows into the subconscious mind, which flows into the Universal Spirit.

A prayer, like the proverbial rose, is the same by any other name. And so it is with the universal source of which we are all inseparable parts. Just as the drop of seawater partakes of all the qualities of the ocean, so do we partake of all the qualities of our Creator.

No one is more worthy than another. Piety can be a pretension. A hasty prayer can be instantly answered. If you are more comfortable on your knees with your head bowed and your hands clasped as you ask for guidance, then by all means follow your desire.

The young minister referred to earlier never bowed his head when he led the congregation in prayer. When he was asked why by a parishioner who was troubled by his apparent lack of conventional piety, he said, "I have what I hope is the requisite humility in the presence of God, but I am not His *humble* servant. He is all around me—and you—an eternal part of us all. I rejoice in my opportunity to serve Him and I wish to lift my head in rejoicing as I pray. If you wish, you may bow your heads; but I wish to look Him in the eye for I have nothing to hide from Him."

The following Sunday more than half the congregation was seen to pray with faces, radiant faces, uplifted.

All that is required of your prayer, you communication with your subconscious, is a clear image of what you want and unquestioning faith—belief that it will be granted to you.

"According to your faith be it unto you," Matthew said.

We may say, "That says it all," and it does. It is the heart of the method we call Imaginology that will lead you to the deep, heartfelt belief in the response of your subconscious that is the key to changing your life.

Nothing helps induce the proper mental attitude so much as the ability to sense your at-oneness with the Universal Spirit. The great problem with the depictions of God that we find on everything from religious postcards to the ceiling of the Sistine Chapel in Rome is that they tend to separate us from our Maker. In depicting God as a separate entity, they remove Him from us and we seem removed from Him.

There is only one way to "visualize" our Maker. That is through our inner senses—through feeling—through a recognition of His miraculous power that has given us the blessing of life, that even now sustains our life and gives us the opportunity to learn.

That is why meditation is so effective. When we quiet ourselves and turn our thoughts to who and what we really are we cannot deny what my beloved grandmother called, "The miracle of We," as she put her blessings on the family.

In earlier pages we spoke of the subconscious mind's tireless effort to keep our bodies operating at peak performance without conscious help from us. It will do so just as long as we do not frustrate and divert it with negative thoughts.

The subconscious mind is God at work. Reinforce that knowledge by closing your eyes and feeling, imagining, the blood coursing through your body, the oxygen going into your lungs and into your blood stream. Imagine the entire miraculous process, the incredible detail of the human machine, and the mind-boggling knowledge the subconscious brings to bear on every single atom and molecule of your being to keep your body in perfect working order.

Perfect working order is what your subconscious is committed to. The only things that will frustrate it are fear, doubt (lack of faith), or deliberate abuse of the principle of cause and effect by the misuse of its power.

Just as you must check your automobile from time to time to make sure it is in perfect working order, check your mental "dip stick" to see if the "oil of your faith" is up to level. If not, refill it with some meditation and prayer. Or, to use another familiar analogy, check your mental battery and give it a quick charge if necessary.

If you will quiet yourself and feel the life force flowing through you—if you will imagine your physical and mental machine working perfectly—you will soon find that it is no problem at all to believe deeply in the miraculous power of the subconscious.

The next step, then, is to pray in perfect faith, without allowing doubt to dilute your prayer, for the good things you wish to materialize in your life.

Then, according to the measure of your faith, those things "will be measured unto you."

Allow not one single shred of doubt to cast a shadow over that truth and you will be using the principle of Imaginology—the simple science of learning to believe.

In doing so you will never need to fear life again, for you will have mastered the art of living under the benevolent protection of the great Universal Spirit of which we, and everything around us, are an inseparable and eternal part.

Some Afterthoughts

Perhaps, because I, too, was a merchant mariner for a while, I am guilty of a special degree of partiality to Joseph Conrad.

I think I know why.

Any man who has stood a watch at sea, huddled behind the bulwarks on the fo'cas'le head, or on the wing bridge, knows the mystic magic of the restless yet curiously peaceful "deep blue" mantle that covers a bit over seventy percent of the earth's surface.

The vessel, throbbing with life, cutting through the sea on a predetermined course, becomes the subconscious mind. The sailor on watch, balancing, responding to each motion, becomes, for a time at least, a fragment of the conscious mind, holding the ship on course, reacting to the vicissitudes of the voyage.

And the sea—it becomes a "reach" of the Universal Source surrounding the sailor and surrounding his ship. There is no greater aloneness, and, yes, no greater at-one-ness unless, perhaps, it is at the 14,000-foot summit of a Mount Whitney or Mount Shasta, where I have also felt this unity with the Universal Spirit.

"The mind of man," wrote Joseph Conrad in *The Heart of Darkness*, "is capable of anything, because everything is in it, all the past as well as all the future."

If you have read this far you know that all the past with its triumphs and tragedies lies in the conscious and in the subconscious mind, the only repositories of accurate history.

That material, those events, are there for any of us to recall, complete with all the lessons implied in them.

It has been said that those who do not learn from history are doomed to relive it. That is as true of us individually as it is of collective mankind.

We can say, "The past is the past; we can't change it." And yet, in a real sense, we can and do change our pasts when we decide to alter the course of our futures. The past would have remained "unchanged" in that its events set the course for the future. But when the course is altered, when we redirect our lives into more positive channels, we have "changed" the past by robbing it of its power to influence us further in a negative way. The wisdom extracted from mistakes changes the past from an impediment to an impeller.

If, after we have demonstrated how we can change our individual lives for the better, we were to apply the chain-letter principle to telling others, very soon we would have several million people believing in the power of "belief."

These people, asking the subconscious to guide our public servants (we forget what they really are!) into the ways of right action, could have a miraculous effect on the quality of our lives in our towns, cities, states, and the country as a whole.

If this sounds hopelessly "far out" or visionary and impractical, stop and think for a moment. We do not have to look any further than the series of recessions that we endure periodically.

When the "Things are too good to be true," state of mind begins to predominate, millions of business people begin to expect a negative reaction. They trim their sails, set out a storm watch, and trail a drogue, a sea anchor, to slow their progress.

Then when the expected economic "storm" strikes, they set out their bow anchors and get ready to ride it out.

But what happens? After they are fed up with the pitching and tossing—and labor is too—they all begin to say, "Things can't get any worse so they're going to get better."

Now they are beginning to reprogram the collective subconscious—and believe. Soon, there is evidence of an upturn. Research and development dollars begin to loosen up. Old machinery begins to get replaced. Production comes up. More product comes into the marketplace. Buyers who were cautious about spending begin to get some of the things they got along without for a while. A general air of optimism begins to pervade the economy; not long after that we all get back to work with a will and we have good times again—until we make the same old mistake by believing that things are too good to last!

Too often the "too good to last" attitude begins right in our own individual lives. Because we do not know who and what we are, and why the good things as well as the bad things happen to us, we revert to our mental "squirrel cages."

If you have understood the supreme simplicity of the principle of mind management, it will no longer be necessary to be trapped again in that self-imposed sentence, that not-so-merry-go-round of positive-negative thought.

It is a lie! Things are never too good to last—except as we believe they are!

Change that belief from negative to positive. *Know that you make the truth by speaking it and believing it*—and, "open sesame!" the truth will indeed make you free.

Don't grab your friends by their lapels or their lavaliers and try to convert them. Twisting arms makes enemies.

The most convincing "act of conversion" takes place when we demonstrate in our own lives, quietly and with dignity, that we can change our circumstances. We become "living proof" and nothing is more convincing than the tried-and-truism, "Action speaks louder than words."

"Gosh, you were lucky, Sam [or Samantha]. How did you do it?"

That's the time to share your knowledge—when it is asked for. That's the only time you can be certain it will be welcome.

Time and time again, mass prayers are held to help someone through an ordeal. I've attended many of them and far too often I have observed that those around me were repeating the words of benediction by rote without really understanding what they meant and what they were intended to do.

How much more effective it would be if our spiritual advisers would take a moment before initiating the prayer to remind us that we must understand the words, their objective and *believe* in both, if they are to reach through the mass subconscious to the intended recipient of the blessings.

Mass prayers, prayed with conviction and understanding, directed to those who make the decisions that shape our nation's future, would "get through" to many of them. It only takes a few convinced men to change a lot of other minds.

I would pray that our lawmakers stop doing the politically expedient things, that they make their judgments unselfishly, and mindful of the public trust, that they come to understand that the support of special interests is a drop in the bucket compared to the support they would get from an electorate that admired their moral courage and their willingness to put service to all above self.

Well, if it is a dream, why not remember that "First comes the dream, then comes the doing?"

So long as a cynical citizenry tolerates political chicanery because "that's the name of the game," then just so long will we continue to fall short of the ideals of our Founding Fathers.

Those men were not afraid to be idealists, to envision a society in which the best in men and women could blossom as an example to the rest of the world's oppressed people.

Neither were they "gods of a sort." They were mortal men, heirs in part to the weaknesses of the flesh, but they knew from experience that the human spirit could not soar to the heights envisioned by its creator in an atmosphere of oppression, selfishness, and greed. They did something about it. The result was the best, freest, most creative society recorded on history's slate, Atlantis and Lemuria notwithstanding!

Change for the good can come. A drop becomes a trickle. A trickle becomes a rivulet. A rivulet becomes a stream. A stream becomes a river and rivers flow to the sea, their original source.

Imaginology, a name for its principle—when it changes one life—initiates that positive trickle.

How much imagination does it really take to envision the sort of world we could all live in if mankind actually did begin to "Accentuate the Positive"?

Index